The Paint Man

My Life in Living Color

by

Joe Cox

with Jeanette Sharp
and David Edwards

The Paint Man, My Life in Living Color
©2013 Joe Cox

Cover Design: Joel Cox Design

Unless noted all scripture references in this publication are from the
New American Standard Version of the Bible.

Printed in the United States of America.

To Dorothy, that cute girl I spotted bouncing a basketball

in the middle of the street fifty-eight years ago. You stole

my heart that day, and I never want it back.

ENDORSEMENTS

"One man with two lives."

When you read this incredible book, you will actually read of one man with two lives. You will read the story of Joe Cox before he met Christ, and of Joe Cox after he became a devoted follower of Jesus. I am so glad to know Joe Cox as a friend and encourager in ministry. In my personal experience, I have only known Joe Cox the committed Christian, whose life bears all the marks of Gospel transformation.

Through reading this book, I have come to know the rest of the story—the story of Joe's life before Christ, and the thrilling story of how he came to find salvation and new life in Jesus. I am so glad to know the whole story—and you will not want to miss a word of Joe's account of his life and walk with Christ. You will also find in this book the story of Joe's loving and faithful wife, Dorothy, and the story of their wonderful family and their life together.

This book represents a great gift to us all—the gift of a man who shares his life story in order that we can all see the work of Christ in his life, in his work, and in his family. I am so thankful that Joe Cox has written his life story. Once you read it, you will be just as thankful. Be warned: Once you start reading this book, you won't be able to put it down.

R. Albert Mohler, Jr., President
The Southern Baptist Theological Seminary
Louisville, Kentucky

"Joe Cox is the American rags' to riches story."

Our state knows Joe Cox as a successful businessman. I know Joe Cox as my Sunday school teacher, encourager and friend. Our Lord and Savior knows' Joe as His child. Joe Cox is an evangelical - I don't mean that as a general category, but as a word to describe his teaching, his conversation, his word, his deeds...his life.

Joe Cox is the American rags' to riches story. Joe is the sinner saved by grace. Example: Abraham had Sara. A nation had Esther. Joe Cox has Dorothy. Without Christ there is no salvation. Without Dorothy, there is no finished story worthy of a book.

This book tells of a present day Old Testament biography. This is a book full of New Testament truths.

Lieutenant Governor Todd Lamb,
State of Oklahoma

"Joe Cox has done us a great favor ..."

In writing The Paint Man, My Life in Living Color, Joe Cox has penned his incredible life's journey and done all who read it a great favor. It's more than a testimony, because its focus is the amazing power of the living God to take a man, who was destined for life's garbage heap, and turn his life inside out.

Every truth Joe shares has been hammered out on the anvil of his own experience.

As a man with a heart for winning lost souls the world over to Christ, I recommend this book to everyone who longs to see how Jesus rewrote the story of a man's life, his family, and his business.

For the Vision,
Tom Elliff
President of the International Missions Board
Former Senior Pastor of First Southern Baptist Church
    Del City, Oklahoma 1985 - 2005
Two term Past President Southern Baptist Convention
www.ibm.org

It was my privilege to serve as Senior Pastor of First Southern Baptist Church Del City, Oklahoma from 1973 to 1985. During that time, Joe and Dorothy Cox became good friends and I came to know them to be not only faithful attendees, but their love for the Lord was evidenced itself in their financial gifts as well as their willingness to serve anytime there was a need and regardless of what that need might be.

If I were to assign a color to Joe, it would, without a doubt, be green. From the time of Joe's conversion experience, he lived his life at full throttle for the Lord. He and Dorothy taught in the Student Ministry Department and worked to influence others to live for Christ.

This book not only provides the reader with the full picture of Joe's life, it also offers lessons he's learned along the journey and includes the difficulties he has encountered.

May God use this book to influence others who may face similar struggles.

Bailey Smith
President Bailey Smith Ministeries
Former President Southern Baptist Convention
www.baileysmith.org
Author of *Real Evangelism, Taking Back the Gospel,*
Real Christianity, Real Christian Excellence and
The Grace Escape.
www.baileysmith.org

ACKNOWLEDGEMENTS

This book's publication process is a story in itself. It is also an answer to prayer. In fact, an answer to many prayers . . . prayers prayed over many years.

At the onset, Dorothy and I knew nothing of the publication process, but we do now. It's been rigorous, formidable, and at times tumultuous. We've shed tears, been forced to relive the difficult seasons of our lives, and been reminded of things we would prefer never saw the light of day. But the concept for this book began in the heart of God. Otherwise, we would have abandoned it long before now.

The writing process can be likened to one of conception and childbirth, because it is a laborious task, and only someone called to write will endure to the end. We pray God uses this work for His glory and to touch the hearts of a multitude, because it is His story, written on the fabric of our lives.

The project began to move forward, when God brought Jeanette and Jim Sharp to visit Quail Springs Baptist Church one Sunday morning. I was in China, so Dorothy sat alone near the aisle. Jim and Jeanette walked down the aisle and took a seat on the pew behind her. It was a divine appointment in the making.

Through their acquaintance, we became good friends. And when Dorothy learned Jeanette was a writer, she told her of our publishing dream, . . . the story of our lives' rocky road history and of God's miraculous, redemptive power. After numerous discussions, we asked her to consider our project, and she asked us for a written copy of our ideas. However, my scribbles, written on a yellow, legal-sized pad, were undecipherable. The project took another step forward when one of my employees, familiar with my scribbles, converted them into a Word document. And with that in place, the manuscript began to take shape. A slow process, which, represents well over a year's work, with periods of highs and lows, setbacks, and edits. But it has been worth every minute.

David Edwards: a talented, multi-published author, whom I had yet to meet, came on board when I learned of his talent and met him one day at our complex's clubhouse. He brought with him a vision for the project we had never dreamed of. But that's part of his talent; gifted beyond measure to think outside the box, and with the ability to see possibilities latent within a project, his contribution to this work is beyond enormous. Without the combined skills, talents, and abilities, of Jeanette and David, this book would continue to be just a dream and a hope held in our hearts. Together, they brought the project to its conclusion and the form you now hold in your hands.

Our dreams, our prayers and our hopes have given birth to, *The Paint Man, My Life in Living Color.*

Dorothy and I also want to thank our sons, Kent, Kirk and Tony, together with their families, whose contribution to our company's success is immeasurable. We are blessed that God placed them in our family and favored us with their care and upbringing.

In addition, we thank the good folks at Lithaprint Inc. for their professionalism, their enthusiasm, and willingness to work with us, and take on our project. It has been our pleasure to meet them, to know them, and to work with them. A relationship we hope will continue as future projects surface.

And last, but by no means least, Jeanette and David thank Dorothy and Joe's crockpot and the good stuff they prepared which thwarted many-a hunger-pang during the long hours of work around their kitchen table. It was much appreciated.

CONTENTS

TELL THE WHOLE VIVID STORY

"It's quite a story."

I've heard that said many times. Probably, because I've told my story many times but never all at once, like I have done in this book. Mostly, I've told my story in pieces and parts in many different places. I've spoken at city clubs and Bible studies; my friend, Tom Eliff, often took me to revivals where he was preaching and had me tell it, and many times evangelist, Bailey Smith, had me share my testimony.

I have lived every moment of my story and I know my conversion is real, because I was there when it happened. My life has been the canvas. Through all of my ups and downs, my all-time highs and lows, God has remained the ultimate Artist; taking all the dark colors and mixing them with the light colors, using the entire spectrum of hues, contrasts, and textures to create a life I never dreamed I'd live.

As I have put my life on paper, one thing became crystal clear to me: "Jesus is still the answer."

Many people are afraid to take a careful look at their selves; while others refuse to even think about their future, because they already know what will happen if they continue on the path they are traveling. To avoid facing the harshness of reality, we play mental tricks on ourselves; it's easier to focus on convenient truth than it is to take an honest look at ourselves.

A look at only the partial places of our lives can generate good feelings about where we are, but it also causes us to miss life's real meaning and message. The truth is, life is messy and filled with ugly details. Filling our minds with selective thoughts about the pleasant creates distracted living, which leads to living by luck as we wait for life to magically go our way.

That's not how it works. It's truth that sets us free. Choosing freedom takes courage, if we are to face life as it really is, in order to arrive at the life God has for us. I cannot gloss over my story, give you half-truths or comfort you with a fairy tale filled with just the high points, but which eliminates the lows.

So here it is, the complete spectrum of me. The darks, the lights, and every hue in between. I hope I've painted a complete and accurate portrait.

Thanks for looking,
- Joe

CHAPTER ONE

PRIMARY COLORS

In the world of paint there are three primary colors: red, yellow, and blue; every color comes from some combination of these basic colors. It is important, both to paint and to life, to learn about these colors and how they interact. As I think about colors in their most basic form and what they mean for life, I've drawn some conclusions.

Red is a powerful color that carries with it many intense emotions, like love, anger, and happiness. It's the heartbeat of passion. It's the drive of our hungers. Red occupies the center of faith.

Blue is the color of trust, loyalty and consistency; it exudes calm and has a sense of renewal. Blue represents water, which brings cleansing and refreshment. Blue is also blue, associated with depression, as in, "I've got the blues today," and has many shades and tones.

> **"Our lives are each a unique mix of colors and textures used to create a life like no other."**

Yellow is bright, cheery, and conveys energy and joy. It's associated with sun, life, and light and brings light into the dark places. It is a warm and inviting color that creates energy.

Color theory goes like this: when one primary color is mixed with another, a secondary color effect is produced, and these are known as complimentary colors, which form the spectrum of all colors.

Our lives are each a unique mix of colors and textures used to create a life like no other. All our experiences of love, loyalty, and life swirl together to form the singular hue that is your specific life. The primary colors of my life were made and mixed by my parents, my siblings, and our beginnings.

Two days before the new year of 1940, Mabel Cox gave birth to me, Joe Tom Cox, her third and youngest child. My dad, Carl, and my mother and older siblings, Jimmy and Jane, lived in the small rural community of Wewoka, Oklahoma located sixty-five miles southeast of Oklahoma City. Wewoka, which means "Barking Waters" in Seminole, was and is the capital of the Seminole Indian Nation,

My Dad as a new car salesman. Usual dress for a salesman was a suit. He is the man in the light gray.

and its name was derived from the sounds made by the small waterfalls east of the early settlement. It is located literally in the center of the United States.

Dad was a new car salesman for Norton Foresee Chevrolet, and as the market for new car sales dwindled in Wewoka, we moved to an area in Oklahoma City known as Capitol Hill. He found work there in the construction industry where he helped build two large water towers located on the north end of Tinker Air Force Base. They remain there to this day.

A WHATEVER-IT-TAKES KIND OF ATTITUDE

On December 7, 1941, "the date that will live in infamy," Japan attacked Pearl Harbor. That day, the world changed and

Front car: Uncle Gilbert & Aunt Thelia. Middle car: My mom & dad, brother Jim, sister Jane & myself. Last car: Uncle Ray & Maureen & son Bobby.

like a ripple effect, things changed at our house too. Dad hitched a small house trailer to our brand-new 1942 two-door, light green Chevrolet coupe; with its bullet-like front end, and prominent grille looking for all the world like a long nose with a mustache under it, and we headed west for California. Over the next few months, that small trailer got even smaller with five people living in it.

Dad was a working-mans man; not afraid to get into the trenches and do whatever it took to get the job done. When we reached Phoenix, he found a job in the construction industry. But for me, the highlight of our time there was when someone gave us a black-and-white spotted puppy. We named him "Pal." A spunky mixed terrier, he never shied away from a fight—in other words, Pal was a lot like me.

As the summer months faded and the holiday season grew near, I had one worry on my young mind: *Our trailer doesn't have a chimney, so how will Santa get in?* Somehow, he managed, and we had a fine Christmas that year.

After a few months in Phoenix, we piled into the Chevy once more and took to the road again with the trailer in tow, this time to Spokane, Washington, where Dad found work at another construction job site.

We didn't put roots down in Spokane, either, because it soon faded from view as we left it behind for Inglewood, California, where Dad landed a job with Northrup America Company. They built airplanes for the war, and we stayed there the longest because Dad had work, at least until the war was over. But Dad's first love was car sales, so on nights and weekends, he pursued that passion, which kept our financial bottom line in the black.

THE PRIMER OF SMALL BEGINNINGS

On occasion, Mom and Dad went out for the evening and when they did, they hired a lady to stay with us. I developed an immediate and intense dislike for her, which bordered on pure hate. When she arrived and they left, I crawled, not under the covers, but under the *bed* to get away from her, and stayed there until my folks returned home. Sometimes I slept there all night. I believe my adamant dislike of her stemmed from the fact that she was one of the few people who made me mind. And I didn't like that one bit. I hated being controlled. An early indicator of what was to come…

I'm the flashy dresser in the white shoes.

I started kindergarten in California, which was my first experience with school of any kind. I rode the bus, and one day something funny happened during the ride home that caused everyone to laugh. That is…everyone except me. Later that evening, I told Mom about the stupid incident, and she asked me, "Did you laugh?"

"No," I said. "I didn't think it was funny." I guess my serious disposition surfaced at an early age, either that or I just had enough sense to know when there was something funny enough to merit a laugh. To do something just because everyone else did it, for the most part, was not who I was.

In those days, the streets were made of tar, which the summer sun turned soft. My friends and I would hunt for a spot where the tar was extra pliable and easy to tear, pull off a hunk, plop it in our mouths, and chew and spit like it was real tobacco. And spit we did, because that stuff tasted *bad*. To live beyond my years was part of my rambunctious personality—I wanted to be older and do the things I saw the grown-ups do, and I wasn't about to let my size or age hold me back.

One day while we waited in the car for Mom, I said, "Watch this." I pushed the cigarette lighter in, pulled it out and touched it to my cheek, and got the surprise of my life. My blood-curdling scream surprised even me. That day, my antics backfired, because unbeknownst to me, Dad had replaced the faulty old lighter with a new one that worked all too well. And the imprint of that lighter is visible to this day.

Then came the day we parked the car outside the Northrup plant and waited for Dad to get off work. And while we waited, we listened to the radio and all of a sudden, the announcer broke into the program and declared, "The war is over!" It was 1945. People started honking their horns and cheering, as everyone entered into outlandish celebrations. That day the somber cloud that had hovered over our world lifted. When Dad got out to the car, Mom told him the good news. In a split-second, he turned on his heels, went back inside the plant and quit his job right then and there.

With the war over, Dad was eager to return to the windy plains of Oklahoma. The red-colored-clay soil found in our neck of the woods flowed through his veins. It was home. That night, we started to pack, made a crate for Pal, and the next day, put him and the rest of our worldly goods on a train headed for Wewoka.

A few days later, we crammed ourselves into the backseat of that same light green, '42 Chevrolet coupe, minus the trailer, which Dad had sold. I thought that car was crowded before, but now, it was really crowded, because we had an additional passenger: my younger brother, Johnny.

> **"Dad was a hard worker, who always managed to find a way to provide for his family, and through his life in action, he taught me to do whatever it took to take care of the household."**

Before we left, Dad hung a canvas bag filled with water on the front bumper to quench our thirst along the way and with that in place, we pulled onto the highway and headed for home. Dad was a hard worker, who always managed to find a way to provide for our family, and through his life in action, he taught me to do whatever it took to take care of the household.

1942 just before we left Wewoka to go to California.

And loving kindness is Yours, O Lord, for You recompense a man according to his work. (Psalm 62:12)

CHAPTER TWO

WEWOKA WISDOM

Once back in Wewoka, seems like the whole town was excited to see us. And I was anxious to see Pal, so we headed over to the train depot to get him. But something must have happened during that train ride from California, because when we approached his crate, he was so riled up no one could handle him. No one, that is, except my godly Pentecostal grandmother, whom we all called Grandma Cox. And from that day on, Pal became her constant companion; wherever she went, Pal went. They were inseparable. A look back over that incident gave me a new perspective. I think Pal must have sensed the peace of God's love in Grandma, so the trauma he experienced on that train ride home just eased right on out of him.

Since I was born in December, school policy didn't allow me to begin first grade until the next year. In that off year, it seemed like I stayed in trouble. An adventuresome tyke, I loved to play pranks on my siblings and neighborhood friends.

The Sharp family lived next door so I often played with their kids, Doug, Rebecca, Grady, and Agnew. We never wanted for something to do which inevitably got us into trouble. Grandma Cox, who lived a block and a half away, had her hands full in her effort to help me stay on the straight and narrow path of good conduct. It proved to be more than a full-time job.

LEARN THE LESSONS THAT LIFE TEACHES YOU

One day the Sharp kids and I were playing in our backyard, and in the blink of an eye, our backyard was ablaze with fire. Its rapid spread soon engulfed the garage, but thanks to the quick response of the fire department, located a block up the street, the blaze was brought under control before too much damage had been done. Since it happened in mid-afternoon, most of the people in our neighborhood were at work and missed the excitement. But it liked to have scared me to death, so much so, that I never played with matches ever again.

On another occasion the Sharp kids and I discovered a new treasure trove; the neighborhood's garbage cans located in the dirt alleyways behind each house. We pilfered through those cans and came across one in which it appeared the owner had emptied his entire medicine chest. Our curiosity with the many colored pills got the better of us, so we consumed them like candy and then moved on to the next adventure of the day.

Grandma Cox and Pal, the dog we got in Arizona.

Later that night, a mysterious sickness set in at our house and at the Sharps. The doctor was called but found himself at a complete loss for a diagnosis. And we were way too sick to be of any real help, but his relentless probe for the source finally jogged our memories. The experience taught me a lifelong lesson: never swallow anything you can't identify, and make sure you know any and all of the possible consequences.

THE RED-HOT REALITY OF ME

The Sharp's grandmother and uncle had a blacksmith shop next to Grandma Cox's house where their uncle Albert shoed horses. He also sharpened plows and lawnmower blades, and as a young boy, the comings and goings at the blacksmith shop—with its variety of activities—held a deep fascination for me. Inside was a fire forge, a place where metal was heated until it was red-hot and then hammered into shape on an iron anvil.

I watched him thrust a worthless piece of metal, held by tongs in his gloved hand, into the midst of the fiery forge until it glowed red-hot. Then he pulled it out, placed it on the anvil and pounded it with his hammer as the sparks flew in all directions. It was as if that metal protested the pounding action of his hammer. But he didn't relent. He kept at it until that metal was the size and shape he wanted.

It was a repetitious process that required time and patience, but when he determined the hammered metal was ready, he plunged it into a barrel of water to cool. Then he straddled the horse's leg, bent it up at the knee, and pulled off the worn horseshoe before he nailed on its new replacement. I loved to watch the Sharp's uncle Albert, to hang around that blacksmith shop, and witness such honest, simple, and yet necessary work.

Though the experience of metalwork is unfamiliar to most people, we still speak of God's work in our hearts as He melts and molds us through His purification process. A process which will ultimately yield positive benefits in an individual's life.

It's not until metal has undergone repeated, rigorous tests under high standards and met strict requirements, can it safely be used. The desired metal must be pure; but in order for it to be pure, it must first go through the fire. It must be melted down and then molded to fit. In the same way, before we can fulfill our purpose, we must be tested under God's standards and purified so we are ready to be used.

While I did not realize it at the time, like that worthless piece of metal, my young life needed to be yielded to the touch of the Master Blacksmith.

"God uses trials and other kinds of experiences to melt us down and recast us into His creation."

Iron sharpens iron, so one man sharpens another.

(Proverbs 27:17)

CHAPTER THREE

THE DAYS THAT SHAPED ME

Compton Grade School was located on the east side of town, where the poor people lived, and it's where I started first grade. Mrs. Turner, my first-grade teacher, also served as the school principal. One day I had done something to get into trouble, so she locked me in her office.

Dial phones had yet to be invented so all calls were routed through a central switchboard located at our local telephone company. When you wanted to make a call, you picked up the phone and the operator said, "Number please." You gave her the number and she made the connection for you. The number for our house was 332, the bank was number 2, and the café was number 18.

First grade. I never was a big smiler.

The day I was locked in Mrs. Turner's office, I picked up the phone on her desk to call Dad. The operator came on the line, but instead of connecting me, she said, "I'm sorry, we're on strike, so I can't help you." In the middle of my plea, in walked Mrs. Turner and boy did I get whipped.

In an effort to defuse the situation, I said, "Mrs. Turner, I need to go to the restroom real bad." Furious, she followed me down the hall, into the restroom, and stood behind me (with her back to me) at the urinal. Embarrassed, my face must have turned ten shades of red. A turn of events I didn't foresee.

VISION DAYS

In the fourth or fifth grade, I hired on to sell the Wewoka Times Democrat Newspaper, and in my mind, no door was off-limits to my entrepreneurial efforts, which included the county and city jails. Up and down Main Street I hawked my wares, "Get your copy of the *Wewoka Times Democrat*, five cents each," I hollered.

We lived seven blocks from Compton School, so I either walked or rode my bike to and from school every day. The funeral home was located at the south end of Main Street, and most days on my way home, I stopped in to take a look at the bodies so I could report to my folks who had died. Sometimes I stuck out a finger and touched the cold, grey-colored corpses just so I could feel what it was like to be dead.

SCHOOL DAYS 1950-51
COMPTON

Learning to smile.

To be sure, there was no vision in those lifeless bodies, which came as no surprise. But sadly, there are many today who are indeed alive but act like dead people.

One of my favorite memories from the fifth grade is Friday nights at the local appliance store. Our house didn't have a television, but the appliance store did and allowed kids to come in and watch wrestling matches. We sat on the concrete floor, eyes glued to the screen, riveted to the action. It was here that I saw vision and passion played out.

Gorgeous George, with his outlandish behavior, riled the audience to a fever pitch when he entered the ring to the strains of "Pomp and Circumstance." His portrayal of a snooty, platinum blonde villain draped in lace and fur outraged the crowd. He strutted around the ring and shouted verbal rebukes at the officials when they attempted to examine him for hidden foreign objects.

Small in size, he made up for it with his boisterous demands. And when the appliance store closed we moved to the sidewalk outside and continued to watch the evening's entertainment through the large plate glass window.

In the sixth grade, all hell broke loose when Compton hired its first male teacher, Mr. Bagley. It was also his first year to teach, and I think he was eager to let every one know how tough he was, because he paddled me at least three times a week. He convinced me, however, who was in charge.

We lived about two blocks from an area of town that contained areas where my friends and I spent a fair amount of time: the railroad tracks, the Wewoka Creek, and a metal scrap-iron company. That last one was where my friends and I played. One of our favorite pastimes was to take the old gas motors off the Maytag washers and nail them to a board. Then we siphoned gas from the junk cars in the salvage lot to get fuel for the motors.

To siphon gas required skill. You stuck a rubber hose into the gas tank and sucked on it, and if you didn't know how to do it, you could suck gas into your mouth quicker than you could say, "Jack Flat." And it burned. But it was pure delight to start up those old motors and listen to their steady hum. While these events seem to be insignificant, they served to create in me the inspiration to succeed and find a way to make things work.

In those days, Wewoka Creek was full of salt water, but that didn't bother us or keep us from swimming in it. We were kids just out to have fun. Back then the Environmental Protection Agency was an ethereal concept whose time was yet to come.

In sixth grade I got my first paper route, and Dad bought me a new black and silver Schwinn Black-Phantom Bicycle complete with a horn, headlights, and taillights. The $85 price tag was a lot for a twelve-year-old in '52, but this began my love affair with beautiful shiny vehicles. I learned something from that new bike: that determination works just like the gears on a bicycle. You can have the state-of-the-art mechanics, but without feet to work the pedals, the gears won't move. To accomplish anything worthwhile requires determination and if we do our part, God will never fail to do His part.

The Schwinn Black Phantom Bike.

GOD DAYS

My first encounter with church happened at the Wewoka Gospel Tabernacle located across the street from our house and Grandma Cox's house. Air conditioners were a thing of the future so in the summer, the windows were left open in hopes a breeze might find its way inside.

> **"To accomplish anything worthwhile requires determination and if we do our part, God will never fail to do His part."**

Those congregants were a lively bunch, whose exuberant style of worship could be heard blocks away. Grandma Cox was a godly woman who attended every service. Her denomination didn't believe you should go to movies or read the funny papers. And women who wore slacks, make-up or jewelry were frowned upon. As a kid who got around town a lot, I saw them shout on Sundays and live bad during the week, and it made me wonder if religion served any real purpose.

Aunt Lill, Grandma Cox's sister-in-law, was my Sunday School teacher. And each year after the Christmas service, kids were given a basket filled with six apples, two or three oranges, a small bag of unshelled-nuts, peppermints, candy canes, and candied orange slices. To us, it was a royal treat.

I don't remember how old I was when it happened. Just that I was pretty young when I went down to the front during a service to get Jesus and be baptized. They said, "All you need to say is, 'Jesus, Jesus, Jesus.'"

In the summer, though, it would get so hot that some of us would take a swim in the church baptistery. Sometimes during revivals, people would go up one aisle, jump into the baptistery, and shout down the other like a bunch of wet dogs. Seems like every time a new preacher came to town, he had a new way to live, but I never did see anyone who lived like Grandma Cox. They all looked like a bunch of flakes to me. From junior high until I was twenty years old, I don't remember going to church more than a time or two.

NEW DAYS

We lived a half-block from Main Street, which meant that I went to town a lot by my self, and although Wewoka was a small town, when I was a kid, it had seven new car dealerships. Dad must have thought the town needed a used car lot, because he put one in our backyard. I loved cars and seldom did a day go by that I didn't pay a visit to the dealerships.

Our back yard. Left to right: '36 Ford, '48 Plymouth, '48 Chevrolet, '50 Chevrolet, and the office in the rear.

Dad kept somewhere between ten and fifteen cars on the lot behind our house. I used to take one of the keys, hide it, and, when it got dark and everyone in the house had gone to bed, sneak out and pick up a carload of my friends. We loved to drive those country dirt roads. I was all of thirteen or fourteen at the time, and unbeknownst to me, even then, God had His eye on me.

WORK DAYS

In the seventh grade, I got a paper route with the *Daily Oklahoman*, the morning paper, and the *Oklahoma City Times*, the afternoon paper. That meant I delivered twice a day during the week, but once on Sunday. Sunday was my biggest delivery day, because I had the combined number of customers from both routes. And since it was a labor-intense day; and delivery began well before daybreak, my sister, Jane, pitched in. She drove the car while I threw the paper. Before long, I hired a couple of friends to help me collect my customer's subscription fees and in addition, bought a Cushman Eagle Motor Scooter, which accelerated the growth of my burgeoning enterprise.

SUMMER DAYS

In the summer between sixth and seventh grade, I went to Idabel, Oklahoma to spend time with one of my Dad's brothers and his wife, Uncle Gilbert and Aunt Thalia. They had cows and horses, but Uncle Gilbert made his living by gambling. He bought a case of cards and Aunt Thalia steamed off the wrappers. Then she marked the cards, and resealed the packages. He always had a partner who knew all the marks.

They had no indoor bathroom facility or tub, so when I wanted to take a bath, I heated water and poured it into a number two galvanized tub. That summer, Uncle Gilbert bought me a new pair of yellow cowboy boots, which made me feel like I was big stuff.

TROUBLE DAYS

Shortly after sixth grade, and on the verge of school's fall semester, my friends told me, "Don't get Mrs. Shantona for your seventh grade homeroom teacher. She's mean and tough." It must have been fate because out of the three-homeroom-teachers, I drew Mrs. Shantona.

She was a Native American and the meanest teacher in school. One day she said, "When God crafted man, He left one in the oven too long and that's where the black man comes from. Another man He took out too soon, and that is the white man. The third one He left in just right and that is the Indian."

Trouble seemed to dog my trail and Mr. Davis, our school Principal, knew just how to handle it. When a teacher sent me down to his office, I knew there was a paddle with my name on it when I walked through his door. So before I went to his office, I detoured out the door, hopped on my motor scooter and headed for home to put baseball pads inside my pants before I returned to Mr. Davis's office to get what I knew waited for me. Since I didn't play baseball, I don't know how I came by those pads, but I sure made good use of them.

Alice Fay Mitchell lived one block from our house. She was in the eighth grade and often brought her friends home with her after school. Girlfriends, that is. They had TV parties, and that's where boys met up with their girlfriend.

PLAY DAYS

In seventh grade I went out for football, but was never very good. That year Dad bought the Oldsmobile dealership and our lives changed in a dramatic way for the better. Mother kept the books and worked out of our house for the next twenty to thirty years. Since Mom was now busy with other things, Dad hired an African-American woman, Ethel Jackson, to keep house and cook for the family, and boy could she cook. Her specialty was brown beans mixed with ground beef; hot out-of-the oven corn bread, and fried pies. Anytime we had that, I thought it was the best meal ever and ate till I could pop.

Ethel's husband, Marcel, was a porter for Dad at the Oldsmobile dealership. He washed and waxed cars, and taught

Cub Scout Football - I am number 45. My dad is behind me. To the left is Mr. Bagley, my 6th grade teacher.

me the intricacies of his job. He had a mouthful of gold teeth and when he smiled, they sparkled like the noonday sun. I liked Marcel.

Every day after school, I headed for the dealership to wash cars. The part of the job I liked best was to take the backseats out of the used cars we traded for and search for any loose change that might have slipped down behind the seats. The dealership was two blocks from our house and halfway in between was Browns Billiards, a pool hall located beneath a clothing store.

I could shoot pool fairly well, but my main love was playing the pinball machine that paid out money. I could go in with two nickels and walk out with two dollars. It was one of the many ways I made extra money to spend. Gas was fifteen cents a gallon and in those days, you could fill a car up for less than four dollars.

CRAZY DAYS

At the end of the workday, when the dealership closed, I made it a point to check all of the cars on the lot to find the one with the most gas in it, and then took the key to that car home with me. Later that night, under the cover of darkness, I'd go back for the car and then find my friends. We drove to the nearest towns, which was either Holdenville, nine miles southeast or Seminole, which was thirteen miles northwest. I was fourteen or fifteen.

One night while we were riding around in Holdenville, I hit a car and didn't stop. By the time I got home, the police were at my house. That late-night joy ride came with a severe lecture, which I hated—I would rather be beaten any day of the week than to endure a lecture.

SCHOOL DAYS 1954-55
WEWOKA

9th grade. Smile is getting bigger.

In the eighth grade, I managed to stay out of Mr. Davis' office. In junior high, Dad said, "Joe, you can do anything you're big enough to do, just don't get caught. And if you do get caught, deny it."

I followed his advice until I was thirty-two years old, and it took me into a lot of places I didn't want to go and cost me more than I ever wanted to pay. Our lives are made up of days, and each of those days contains lessons and principles we are to learn. The goal in each of our days is to let go of the bad and take hold of the good. Be a quick learner of God's truth. It's a far better way to learn something than it is to learn it the hard way.

It can be difficult to accept correction, but a wise person will receive it. Emotional obstacles will crop up which will keep us from the truth such as feelings of condemnation, embarrassment and a defensive attitude. To make progress in life, we must admit our faults and take action to change our ways. If we are ever to be of any use, we must allow the correction to work in us.

A rebuke goes deeper into one who has understanding than a hundred blows into a fool. (Proverbs 17:10)

CHAPTER FOUR

PAINTED ON MY HEART

Prayer is like the scarlet thread Rahab hung out her window: it identified her desire to be spared when Israel's army captured Jericho, the city she called home. I believe it was Grandma Cox's prayers woven throughout my childhood and young adulthood that spared my life. Prayer is powerful in that God not only hears our prayers, but our prayers continue into perpetuity: they never cease or weaken in their effect on our behalf for all of eternity. That's a mighty long time.

> **"Joe, someday, you will serve God."**

Grandma Cox was five feet tall and had hair that came down past her knees, which she wore up in a bun. I never saw her in anything other than long dresses and black "old lady" shoes. She lived up the street from us, and from seventh grade through my high school years, her house pretty much became my second home.

Grandma Cox studying her Bible.

The time I spent with Grandma Cox made an indelible impression on me. When she wasn't busy in the kitchen or doing household chores, I could find her in her rocking chair reading the Bible. She often said, "Joe, someday, you will serve God." At the time, I just couldn't see it. But she did, even without her glasses.

Back Row L to R: Grandpa Cox, Aunt Rosy, Grandma Cox, Maureen, My Mom, My Dad. Front Row: Bobby, Jimmy, Jane and Myself.

Those glasses proved to be a constant source of frustration for her because she couldn't keep track of them. "Where are my glasses? Has anyone seen my glasses?" was her oft-repeated phrase, because without them, she was at a loss to read.

But they were an easy find for me. "Grandma, they're on top of your head."

She loved Dr. Pepper and sweet tea. And Grandma's sweet tea was sweet. She kept a quart jar of that sugary liquid on the top shelf of her refrigerator; and with one glance, I could spot at least three inches of sugar settled at the bottom.

Grandma didn't own a TV, but she did have a radio. And we never missed Thursday night's program schedule; which included *Dragnet,* with Jack Webb. He played the lead role of Sergeant Joe Friday, a Los Angeles County Police Detective. The announcer, George Fenneman, began each episode with: "Ladies and gentlemen, the story you are about to hear is true."

Other catch phrases included: "We were working the day watch," and "Just the facts, ma'am, just the facts." And Mr. Fenneman never failed to remind the listeners: "The names you are about to hear have been changed to protect the innocent," which further escalated the suspense. The realistic sound effects and storyline held me captive. Afraid I might miss something: I sat in rapt attention and listened as Sergeant Friday and his partner, Joe Gannon, played by Harry Morgan, caught the bad guys. Sometimes I got so caught up in the story, I sat with the covers over my head, scared to death until it was over.

Just as I had heard Sergeant Friday say many, many, times, "Just the facts." It would be what my grandmother taught me that would be forever painted on my heart.

LOVE GOD. WORK HARD

Grandma's house had open-flame stoves in every room. The one-inch-by-ten-inch walls were constructed of single-ply boards covered with cheesecloth and wallpaper. In order to

The Harris Family - my Mom with the raised collar.

survive the frigid Oklahoma winters, each of the thin-walled rooms required an open stove. Otherwise, the room's occupant would freeze to death.

As I think back over those times, it's a wonder we weren't all asphyxiated from the fumes. But Grandma's strong faith in God's good-hand of provision upon us, never gave her a moment's pause for concern. Because to her: God was alive, and her faith was alive, and her life was a living testimony of His love for the world to see.

She rented out rooms in her house to help pay the bills, a fairly common practice in those days. One of her renters drank a case of cokes every week and never bothered to return the empty bottles. So Grandma Cox gave them to me for disposal. In my mind's eye, each returned bottle had an invisible worth of two cents stamped on it, which meant that a returned case was worth almost a half-dollar. The entrepreneurial spirit in me; ever on the look out for ways to earn extra money, spotted another source of revenue, so I was happy to take them off her hands. Never underestimate the value of a penny.

Laziness brings trouble to the soul as well as other areas of life. The honest way is the only way. To create and sustain success, one must embrace these bedrock principles.

The way of the sluggard is as a hedge of thorns, but the path of the upright is a highway. (Proverbs 15:19)

My grandparents on my mother's side, Sid and Tennie Harris, lived on a farm north of Seminole, Oklahoma. They were sharecroppers, and never in their lives did they own a piece of property or the house where they lived.

Granddad Sid lived to be 95 years old. A smoker, he rolled his own cigarettes until age 90, at which time he abruptly quit.

My brother, Jim, asked him one day, "Why did you quit smoking, Granddad?"

He replied, "I've smoked long enough and just figured it was time to stop."

I loved to visit Grandmother Harris' house: we played in the barn, climbed on haystacks, and gathered eggs, which was a welcome change from life in Wewoka. Summer visits at their place included swims in the water troughs, which Granddad used to water his animals. The troughs were made of concrete and if we wanted to go for a swim, we had to first clean them out.

Life on the farm was full of hard work. Nothing came easy: but, while I was there, I learned that diligent toil combined with the blessing of the Lord made succeeding in life's tasks a little easier.

Their house didn't have electricity, so oil lanterns provided their light. And

> **"I learned that that diligent toil combined with the blessing of the Lord made succeeding in life's tasks a little easier."**

Granddad loved to listen to boxing over their battery-powered radio. Later in his life he watched championship wrestling on TV and if you told him it was fake, he got mad. We never did convince him it wasn't real.

FIND JOY IN THE SIMPLE THINGS

Sunday dinners at Grandmother Harris' house were a treat, though her delicious fried-chicken dinners were never an easy task. It started with a chicken chase in the backyard to catch three or four of the feathered fowls. Once caught: she wrung their heads off, drained their blood and dropped them into a big, cauldron-sized pot filled with boiling water. After the feathers were soggy and loose, she plucked them off by hand. It was a smelly job. Then she washed them, took them into the kitchen and cut them into pieces.

Before the pieces were ready for her frying pan, she coated them with flour, which sealed in the moisture and made the chicken crusty—and also served as a base for her gravy. And no meal was complete without her biscuits. Grandmother Harris' fried chicken, biscuits, and gravy dinner was a culinary delight, pure and simple. The drumstick was my favorite piece.

Sunday's around Grandmother Harris' table remain among some of my favorite memories. We ate fried chicken and talked and laughed about life on the farm. As I reflect on those times around that table, it was there that I began to understand that happiness must be heart-deep or it is nothing at all.

A joyful heart is good medicine, but a broken spirit dries up the bones. (Proverbs 17:22)

Mom told me that in my grandparent's era, children ate last not first. And another common practice was the multiple use of dishes: since Granddad sopped his plate clean, the first one behind his chair got to use his somewhat-clean dish when it came time for them to eat.

My grandparents were God-fearing, churchgoing people, whose way of life included hard work. Their children held them in great esteem, and they in turn conducted themselves with dignity and integrity. In spite of their hardships and meager holdings, every one of their children earned college degrees: a tribute to their godly upbringing.

What we learn early in life, we do not forget later in life. Proverbs 22:6 has always meant a lot to me: and the word, "train," used in that passage, literally means "to taste." When I worked with my grandparents: I simultaneously received a taste of godly character, which leads to good choices and our choices, over time, become second nature. They were good, life-long lessons planted in my soul for the rest of my life.

Train up a child in the way that he should go, even when he is old he will not depart from it.   (Proverbs 22:6)

CHAPTER FIVE

DANGER AHEAD!

One afternoon, I went by Alice Fay's house and spotted this cute girl bouncing a basketball in the middle of the street. Her name was Dorothy Garrett, and while she caught my attention, I didn't catch hers. In fact, she wouldn't give me the time of day—but little did she know that some day she would become my wife.

Wewoka High School included grades nine through twelve: a decided change for me from junior high, where I was top dog. Freshmen were the new kids on the block and I felt out of place . . . yet somehow I was elected class president the first semester. It was a mystery to me.

One day in 1955, after a big spring rainstorm, some of us went to Wewoka Lake to watch a gigantic amount of water pour over the spillway. On the way back to town: I saw a couple of my older brother's friends put a small boat in Wewoka Creek, which had overflowed its banks. They said, "A friend's going to pick us up at Broadway of America," which was a road six miles to the east.

It was around three o'clock in the afternoon when I got into that boat with Dwayne Boyd and Wiley Toomie. And by the time we reached the road where the guy was supposed to meet us, he was nowhere to be found. Without oars: we were at the mercy of wherever the current took us, but we got back into the boat anyway and went on to Wetumka, another five or six miles.

THE WEWOKA TIMES

Entered at Wewoka, Okla., postoffice as 2nd class mail under act of March 3, 1879.

FOURTEEN PAGES   WEWOKA, OKLAHOMA, SUNDAY, MAY 22, 1955   PRICE 5c

etumka Boat Search

e the first to travel was almost a success port that they called the emergency crew A, 171st Field Artil- d been mobilized to ...

20, launched a metal north of Wewoka at ed up Joe Tom Cox, ening near the bridge. rip even though they miles away. But the the crow flies, the

rt had been told that if le the trip to Wetumka eoka via the water route, d have covered 120 miles. ered they floated 90 mil- celling the excursion off. after 10 p.m., law en- l officers, the Boat Club's y crew, complete with hooks and motor boats, national guard battery, biliting for a search of d creek bottoms. ye came into town before h actually started. Shell and Gordon Ander- both offered to fly their planes in the search in bad weather. fifteen of the national it had assembled at the and were preparing to

NAVIGATORS POINT OUT COURSE—Trio of Wewoka youths who were almost successful in navigating flood-swollen Wewoka creek from Wewoka to Wetumka Friday night look over a map of Oklahoma showing the route they took. Looking over the route are Wiley Twomey, Duane Boyd and Joe Tom Cox. (Staff Photo)

Intelligence System Probed

Mark Clark Heads Investigative Body

West German Leader Maps Plan for Fast Rearmament Program

BONN, Germany, May 21—UP—Chancellor Konrad Adenauer Saturday mapped an all-out drive to rearm West Germany quickly in an apparent effort to nip a Soviet campaign to neutralize Germany.

Israel-Egypt Border Erupts

Mortars, Artillery Machine Guns Roar

Gary Seeking Lawmakers' OK On Auto Bill

Law Meant to Aid Oklahoma's New Car Dealership Firms

OKLAHOMA CITY, May 21—UP — A bill pitting used car dealers against new car dealers shoved to the center of the legislative stage Saturday by Gov. Raymond Gary, who called for passage of the bill in the closing days of the session.

The legislative windup, which leaders hope will come next week, unexpectedly will have the bill broadening the excise tax on automobiles as a major issue in the final days.

Gary said Saturday he wants the bill passed as a protection to new car dealers, although Attorney General Mac Q. Williamson issued an opinion indicating that the bill would be illegal if the legislature quits next week. Williamson said it is a revenue measure which must lie on the governor's desk five legislative days before adjournment.

The bill would require payment of the two per cent excise tax within ten days on new cars transported into Oklahoma and sold by used car dealers. New car dealers want it passed as a means of cutting competition from the used car lots.

Fails By One Vote

Grand : Delivere Remains

A grand jury peti- mitted to District Judg urday. But the questic lated it and delivered it tery as when rumors c two weeks ago.

Since the petition been unable to determ names of the circulators the petition would tal. agreement that "you

★ ★ ★

Text of Grar Jury Petitior

Five Items liste For Investigatio

Here is the text of t jury petition to District J Howell Saturday:

"We, the undersigned cit resident taxpayers of County, Oklahoma pursu provisions of Article II, of the Constitution of the Oklahoma request and that a Grand Jury be con der the statutes and lav State of Oklahoma in a

When darkness settled, we couldn't see a thing around us, let alone where we were going. I thought to myself, *Joe, you're going to drown*. Soaked clean through; and shivering from the cold, somehow, through the pitch-dark night we saw the glimmer of a light coming from a house about a half-mile a way. Using our hands as oars, we managed to maneuver the boat close to the bank and grabbed on to a fence post that was anchored to dry ground and climbed out. We walked the fence line toward the light, and a couple of miles beyond that found the highway.

From there we hitched a ride with a guy who let us out on Main Street in Wewoka at about ten o'clock. The guy, who was supposed to pick us up, had gotten scared and contacted the police. Fearing the worst, they called out the National Guard and mobilized a search party. My folks and everyone else in town thought for sure we were dead. Later I learned that even my sister, worried and distraught, raced around the house shouting, "Joe's dead!"

So when I showed up that night, everyone was very happy to see me alive, even my sister. Earlier that afternoon when I got into that boat with Dewayne and Wylie, I had no idea of the perilous situation that lay ahead of me.

Every path we choose already has a destination and our decisions propel us down that path. Often we don't think about the outcome before we start a journey—we just do what seems right at the moment without thinking about the consequences. But it's wise to pause a moment and ask ourselves, "If I stay on the path that I am on, will it lead to the outcome I really want?" I had to learn that the hard way.

There is a way which seems right to a man, but its end is the way of death. (Proverbs 16:25)

CHAPTER SIX

MAN IN THE MAKING

On March 1, 1955, my good friend Gary Cluck and I joined the National Guard. We signed up for a stint of four years plus another three in the reserves, and were assigned to the 171 Field Artillery Division. Gary was fourteen and I was fifteen. In order to join, we had to lie about our ages, but we thought it was worth it. The Guard met on Monday nights once a month, and every August they shipped us to Fort Hood, Texas for a two-week summer camp.

We left Wewoka on a Saturday morning, and rode in the back of a two-and-a-half-ton truck until Sunday afternoon, when our military transport pulled into Fort Hood. At the crack of dawn Monday, we took our 105 Howitzers out to the practice field and fired them for the better part of day. I think the reason I wear hearing aids today is due to the loud boom those Howitzers made every time they were fired. Ex-Korean war vets trained us, and by the end of my seven-year military obligation, I received an honorable discharge and earned the rank of SSgt E5.

The Guard taught me many things among which was discipline . . . something I had never learned, but needed in the worst way. And KP duty was not for those with a squeamish stomach, because the worst part about the assignment was the grease trap. It had to be cleaned, and the stench from that trap was putrid enough to make a grown man with a stout stomach puke.

One of the main components of basic training was marching, which seemed to have no end. But the Guard had a purpose for everything they assigned. Compliance with orders was a crucial part of our training if we were to be prepared for combat should a crisis or another war develop. Before it was over, we marched with precision and worked as a unit as each man fulfilled his role.

We either marched or picked up debris around the base grounds. The Guard demanded order and meticulous maintenance: from my boots, to my bed, to the latrines, and the base grounds. Slothful behavior was not tolerated. Regardless of the project, the Guard had perfected the way they wanted it done down to a science.

While in the Guard, I made many lifelong friends. And much of what I learned throughout my time there still impacts my life today; like the orderliness and discipline that shows up today in the way I like things neat, clean, and in order.

Get rid of pointless pursuits and distractions. Use your work to enlarge your thought life and spiritual life. Focus your energy on things that will make you successful in life, and you'll find that you will enjoy a richer, more satisfying life—even in the unpleasant aspects your work might often require.

He also who is slack in his work is brother to him who destroys. (Proverbs 18:9)

Left to Right: Myself, Gary Cluck, Don Cole (Best Man in my wedding), my brother Jimmy.

CHAPTER SEVEN

ROLLER MARKS

Around this time, my sister, Jane, worked as a telephone operator. She used part of her wages to purchase a new blue-and-white Oldsmobile 88, all fins and prominences, which she let me use for dates. Morgan's Mug—a popular eatery owned by the parents of professional golfer Gil Morgan—was one of my favorite places to take my dates. Their steak-sticks, fries, and fresh pies were mouth-wateringly wonderful; banana cream was one of my favorites. Two people could eat at Morgan's Mug for two dollars, and have enough money left over to take in a movie.

Dad's Hamburgers was another favorite place to eat. In fact, I ate lunch there almost every day. A burger and slice of pie (cherry was another of my favorites) cost fifty cents.

THE RACE NOBODY WINS

At the time, '56 Fords, like the two-tone, forward-leaning Crown Victoria or the hulking, nothing-but-muscle Thunderbird, were considered to be hot cars which guys liked to drag race. The key to a drag race was for the driver to hold the brake down with his left foot and the accelerator with his right foot. When the signal to begin the race was given, the driver released

the brake, but maintained a full throttle on the accelerator. The guy that had an automatic transmission under his hood had the advantage over a standard transmission, because he didn't have to shift gears.

One night some guys from Seminole, a town about ten miles away, came to Wewoka in search of someone to drag with. I went to Dad's dealership and "borrowed" a new, all-white '56 Oldsmobile 88 with a stick shift from the showroom floor. Then drove to the intersection at Second and Mekusukey (pronounced Mek-a-sookey), The guys from Seminole pulled up along side me, and we positioned our cars to head south. Another guy stood to our left and when he lowered his arm, we burned rubber. And that Olds looked for all-the- world like a great white shark ready to take out a seal. But a block down the road, when I shifted from second to third, I must have hit reverse because the transmission blew up.

When I got out of the car, oil gushed like a geyser all over the street from a big hole inside the transmission. We pushed the car back to the dealership and into the mechanic's section, because I sure couldn't put it back on the showroom floor with it leaking oil like a sieve. The next day, I knew I was in big trouble, so I didn't go to work. When Dad got to work and assessed the damages, he called the house and said, "Joe, did you take the new car off the showroom floor last night?"

Scared and embarrassed, I confessed my folly. He grounded me for a month and prohibited me from driving any of the dealership's cars. This was one time when Dad's advice—do anything you are big enough to do, and if you get caught, deny it—didn't pay off. I was to blame and I hated how it made me feel. I never did it again.

Folly means foolishness, and there is nothing worse than an old fool. All the years of recklessness become more obvious as time goes by. It is important to gain understanding early in life so your years are lived in the right direction. Thankfully even in our craziest moments, God will not leave us alone. He will use our foolish choices to get us back on the right track—and *off* the oil-slicked, racetrack.

Folly is joy to him who lacks sense, but a man of understanding walks straight. (Proverbs 15:21)

CHAPTER EIGHT

TESTING LIFE

In tenth grade, though I wasn't the greatest athlete, I tried out for the school basketball team. The coach, Mr. Keddy, asked me, "What do you think you're doing, Joe?" He knew I couldn't run because he bummed cigarettes from me in the janitor's room. I ran the steps that day and puked my guts out. He was right. It wasn't for me.

My friend Raymond Cain and I were in the same biology class, and the two of us were hard-pressed to get a passing grade. A test was in our all-too-soon future, which we had to pass, but as luck would have it, I had secretly observed Mr. Drake hide his copy of the test. During study hall I went to his room, which was empty and locked.

But that little wrinkle posed no problem for me since I had a key to everything—because I had stolen it from the janitor's room where we smoked. I unlocked the door; hurried to the front of the room, retrieved the copy of the test, and had it in hand, when I heard someone rattle the doorknob as if to open it. I ran to the closet and flattened myself on the floor; Mr. Drake came in, opened the closet door, looked around, and left. Scared to death, my heart pounded like a base drum at halftime. I couldn't believe he didn't see or hear me.

Raymond and I passed the test, but Mr. Drake commented later that he thought someone had managed to take a copy. Maybe he *did* see me after all . . .

Mr. Drake also kept a pickled pig in a quart fruit jar on a shelf in his classroom. I swiped it and stored it in the glove compartment of my car just so I could show people what a pickled pig in a jar looked like. As I look back on the incident now, I regret taking that pig, but it may have influenced my decision to join the Future Farmers of America (FFA). Although my motive to join at the time was just to get a much-needed good grade, that decision had built-in life lessons, I could never have foreseen.

TAKE RESPONSIBILITY

As part of the FFA: I bought a Chester White pig, rented a place to keep him, and fed and groomed him every day. I showed him at the county fair and then again at the big spring stock show in Oklahoma City. For three years I did this and had a lot of fun, but that pig was never the grand champion I hoped for.

Never before had I been responsible for a living thing that depended solely upon me for its sustenance. And in the process of caring for and raising that pig, I gained something more valuable than a grand champion: I learned responsibility, a character quality that would last me a lifetime.

God will make your life work if you will take responsibility for your choices. You have one life to live, so decide to take responsibility for it and do the thing He has called you to do. Once you make the decision to follow Him, even if you've stolen test answers or pickled pigs, He'll honor your choices and walk with you every step of the way.

Commit your works to the Lord, and your plans will be established. (Proverbs 16:2)

CHAPTER NINE

THE COLOR OF LOVE

The summer between my sophomore and junior year, a couple of friends who had just graduated high school needed a ride to Norwood, Colorado. They had signed on to work for a logging mill and promised to get me a job too, if I would drive them up there. I told Mom and Dad I was headed to work in the wheat harvest of western Oklahoma.

Carrol Cain, John Scott, and I left town in my maroon-colored, '48 Chevrolet coupe bound for Colorado. This car was a little bit sleeker than the '42 Coupe we'd driven out West when I was younger, and the maroon paint job gave its subtle curves a lot more style. My friends got jobs driving logging trucks, while I was assigned to a DC-6 Caterpillar pulling logs. We lived in a cabin out in the woods, and the sole source of our water came from the creek behind the cabin, whose waters were ice cold. If you wanted to bathe, you had to heat the creek water on the stove and pour it into a number-two galvanized tub. Carrol and John were both over 6 feet 5, and to see them in a number-two tub was a sight to behold.

I worked the job, but after about a month, I got homesick for Wewoka. It was the first time I had been away from home that long, and I was ready to sleep in my own bed and see my folks again. One morning I said to Carrol and John, "I'm going back to Wewoka today. If you guys want a ride, get in." They declined my offer and stayed on through the rest of the summer.

On my way home, I approached the Royal Gorge Bridge, which at the time was the world's highest free suspension bridge, spanning the Arkansas River at a height of 1,053 feet. I had never driven in the mountains alone before, and the height of that bridge scared me to death. But across that bridge was my route home, as well as my folks, and the love of my life; so armed with a white-knuckled grip on the steering wheel, and fear and trepidation in my heart, I drove that '48 Chevy across the bridge. Only God knows how scared I was and the great relief that swept over me when I reached the other side.

I arrived home in time for the football season of my junior year; and the hot-looking gal I met at Alice Fay's back in the eighth grade, Dorothy Garrett, finally agreed to go out with me. We went to the Wewoka vs. Seminole game and that night at the first kiss, I knew I was in love. Dorothy was a senior and I was a junior; she was a straight-A student, while I struggled for C's

My first date with Dorothy.

and D's. Every afternoon I took her home from school where she spent the next hour or two deep in her studies.

Dorothy was studious while I was the exact opposite. During all my school years, I never took a report card home and was never held accountable for any part of my academic performance. But the highlight of my junior year was being with Dorothy, which made it one of the most enjoyable years of my life.

MY HEART IS FULL

In the summer between my junior and senior year, I took a job on a road gang, which worked between Wewoka and Bowlegs. We laid asphalt, (by this point in my life, I had learned to *make* the street and not *chew* it.). Before the asphalt was laid down, the surface edge had to be swept, and that was my job; pushing a broom along the edge of the road. That asphalt was beyond hot as was the summer sun, which scorched everything under its rays. This rugged work required a herculean effort to make it through the day, but it was still worthwhile. That summer Dorothy moved to Tulsa and enrolled in Drauns Business College.

Senior year was uneventful for me, because Dorothy was in Tulsa. I missed her so much I'd drive to Tulsa several times a week; a one-way trip of almost a hundred miles, then go back on Friday night to get her and bring her home for the weekend, then drive her right back to Tulsa on Sunday night. That racked up a lot of miles on my car, but I didn't mind, because it also put a song in my heart.

Happiness for me was being with Dorothy.

Love is the best thing we can commit our life to, and can be expressed in many

Photo from a valentine banquet. I don't know who tied my tie.

different ways, but the one constant in love is that it always gives. Even now, I look for ways to show Dorothy how much I love her. God wants us to color each other's world.

O satisfy us in the morning with Your loving kindness, that we may sing for joy and be glad all our days.

(Psalm 90:14)

CHAPTER 10

CHANGE OF INTENSITY

In December of 1957, my sister, Jane, took me to Samuel Gordon Jewelry store where I bought Dorothy a $500 engagement ring, paid for with my National Guard check. Jane was the host at a New Year's Eve party in Oklahoma City, and Dorothy and I were invited. That night I gave Dorothy the ring and asked for her hand in marriage. She said, "Yes."

A month later, in the middle of January, we found out Dorothy was pregnant. I was a senior in high school with no money and washed cars at my dad's auto dealership. The

Our one and only wedding picture taken February 15, 1958. Joan, Dorothy, myself and Joe Don Cole.

pregnancy didn't upset me though, because I loved Dorothy, wanted to marry her and spend the rest of my life with her. But I was worried and concerned, however, about how we would make ends meet.

Nevertheless, we married on February 15, 1958 in a simple ceremony that took place in the basement of the First Baptist

Church of Wewoka. Mom and Dad attended our wedding along with Dorothy's parents. Pastor Frank Elkins officiated, and our friends, Joan Franklin and Joe Don Cole, stood up with us. Besides these few people, there was also a man with a small camera, who snapped a few pictures of our humble event.

Dorothy was a beautiful bride, but there were no funds for wedding frou-frous. There were no flowers, no wedding cake, no bowl filled with frothy pink punch. There was no white, laced-covered wedding gown with a sweeping train, nor a sweet little flower girl to drop red rose petals down the aisle. In fact, there was no music to mark the occasion, except the music that joined our hearts together. We were two young people caught by the consequences of our choices, in love but afraid and uncertain as to what to do next.

I painted my maroon colored Chevy Coupe charcoal grey in honor of our special day. It was about the only thing I could do. The new paint job and color change—plus a lot of elbow grease—made that car look like a new one.

After we were married, Dorothy left Tulsa and moved back to Wewoka where we lived with my parents in their two-bedroom house. It forced my younger brother, Johnny, to sleep on the living room sofa. But my thoughts were preoccupied with the medical expenses headed our way from an imminent childbirth, and my desperate need to find a job.

As a couple, we leaned on each other and that was what got us through those difficult times. In your marriage give your issues to God and don't pick on each other's weakness, but participate in each other's strengths. Honor the choices you've made; accept whatever consequences might come from them, and work together in unity to build something beautiful together.

For this cause a man shall leave his father and his mother, and shall cleave to his wife; and they shall become one flesh. (Genesis 2:24)

CHAPTER ELEVEN

A LIFE WITHOUT COLOR

In May 1958, now a new husband and expectant father with a wife halfway through her pregnancy, I wrote a letter to Uncle Cyrus Gordon, my dad's sister's husband, and ask for a job. A welder, Uncle Cyrus traveled all over the country and at the time, he and Aunt Marie were working a job down in Karnes City, Texas. After reading my letter he contacted me and said, "Sure, Joe, you can work for me as a welder's helper." So with the promise of a steady income, the week before my graduation ceremony, Dorothy and I headed south in my '48 Chevrolet coupe.

Star Motel, Karnes City, Texas.

Karnes City is located just north of San Antonio, down near San Marcos, Texas. Upon arrival we rented a room at the Star Motel, the same place where my aunt and uncle lived. It was one room with a small kitchen. Dorothy had been a straight-A student in school: but when it came to the kitchen, she didn't know how to boil water, so Aunt Marie taught her how to do that and much more—she taught her how to cook. Each morning Dorothy packed a lunch for me, then Uncle Cyrus and I drove five miles on dirt roads out to the middle of a field to weld flanges on pieces of pipe. The temperature outside was 100°F in the shade.

While it wasn't my favorite type of work, I had a pregnant wife and was thankful for the job. It was the first time we had been away from our families and both of us were a little homesick. The Karnes' project lasted about seven weeks, after which we followed Uncle Cyrus on to Mt. Vernon, Missouri for the next job.

On the way to Missouri, I traded my narrow '48 Chevy for a wide and spacious '54 Oldsmobile 88 with a blue top and a white bottom, which looked more like a speedboat than a hunk of Detroit muscle. In Mt. Vernon, we rented an old, one-car garage that had been converted into an apartment. The place was so cramped that the landlord had to put the small refrigerator in the bathroom. You could use the toilet and eat out of the refrigerator at the same time. Not an ideal beginning.

One night as Uncle Cyrus welded, the bright glare from his torch crept around the open-ended sides of my protective eyewear and scorched my eyes. In an instant I was blinded and fear gripped my heart. I wasn't sure if I would ever be able to see again.

What if this blindness was permanent? What would happen to Dorothy and our baby yet to be born? How would I provide for them? These anxious thoughts and more raced rampant through my mind, and taunted me with uncertainty. Frightened and alone in the darkness, my world was colorless. After close to twenty-four hours, the dark curtain over my eyes began to recede and gradually, my sight returned. And with its return, my heart filled with gratitude.

Even in the dark there is power in love. Learn to trust God when you are afraid. Sometimes we have to face life and "do it afraid," but God will give you the courage to face your fear and push through it, no matter what may happen to you.

For God hath not given us the spirit of fear; but of power, and of love, and of a sound mind. (II Timothy 1:7)

CHAPTER TWELVE

PAINTING A NEW LIFE

Most of my friends were older than me; and after graduation, many of them had moved to Odessa, Texas to work in the oil fields, leaving me behind. At that time, the petroleum industry in the Midwest was in a boom, and I liked what I saw. My friends drove new cars, had cash in their pockets, and urged me to join them. So Uncle Cyrus and I parted ways and I headed to Texas, where I hoped to earn enough money to provide for my family. Dorothy, meanwhile, went back to Wewoka to live with my parents in a more pregnant-friendly environment.

Halliburton, a company that operated out of Midland, hired my friend Raymond and me to work a job in Monahans, Texas, which was about thirty miles west of Odessa. We drove a bulk cement truck and a sand truck to well sites for cementing and fracking. Raymond and I shared a two-room shack.

I was homesick for Dorothy, so when she dropped the casual comment, "I might have the baby this weekend," during a phone call on October 16, that was all I needed to hear. I drove all night to get back to Oklahoma. She entered the hospital around 1 o'clock in the morning and Kent was born close to noon October 17, 1958. He was a beautiful baby with lots of dark hair, and the total cost of the delivery and hospital expenses came to a whopping $165.

Neither of us had a lick of experience when it came to babies. And in those days, hospital policy didn't allow anyone other than the nurse's staff to touch the baby for the first few days. I was young, awkward, and unprepared for this new fatherhood role, and Kent didn't come with a set of instructions, so I couldn't see the blind spots. Like a fish out of water; I felt isolated, out-of-place, and useless, so I went to a football game that night in Ada. And on Monday, I returned to Monahans and rented a house for Dorothy and Kent.

Dorothy stayed in Wewoka with Kent until December, at which time I brought them down to Monahans to live with me. While his colic and crying made for many a sleepless night for her, aside from that, he was a mild-mannered, good baby.

One day after I left for work, Dorothy launched a search for a better house. When I came home that night, I was shocked to find that not only had she found us a better house, she had moved us in. Since the new house was already furnished, there wasn't much to move other than our personal items. I had to admit, her house selection was a considerable improvement over mine.

That year was our first Christmas in our new home and away from our families, and it made us appreciate the little that we did have. Monahans had a five-and-dime store, so I scoured their shelves in search of something we could put on our scrawny tree, and returned with angel hair, tinsel, and Christmas tree lights. We were thankful for our tree with its scanty decorations, we were thankful for each other, and our hearts held hopes for a brighter future.

Life is not perfect. Some things, in any event, need to be fixed. The reality is that there are some things that wealth can't fix. It can't keep trouble, disappointment, or pain from your door. Wealth can provide shelter, clothes, and food, but wealth can't heal a broken heart, which is why we must look to God as our source, and be thankful for His presence.

THANKFULNESS IS A CHOICE

Thankfulness is a powerful attitude, because it gives us strength to endure the unexpected situations in life. A thankful spirit is created when we recognize and choose to make a big deal out of little blessings. I have found plenty in my life to be thankful for and so can you, if you will look for it. Begin and end each day with thankfulness, it's a good thing to do, because whatever you concentrate on will at some point overtake your vision of the future. If your sole focus is on your problems, they will appear bigger than they really are: but if you focus on the good things, that's what you will tend to see, which will lead you to a happier, healthier, more peaceful life.

Better is a little with the fear of the Lord, then great treasure and turmoil with it. (Proverbs 15:16)

CHAPTER THIRTEEN

LIFE TESTS US EVERYDAY

I loved to work overtime, because it meant a boost in my paycheck at the end of the month. Anytime I could get it, I was first in line to volunteer for the extra hours, and $115 per week looked mighty good to me.

ENDURE THE STORM

Some of my Wewoka friends had jobs with Welex, a perforating company in Odessa, and they encouraged me to apply, which I did. Welex hired me, so we moved once more, this time from Monahans to Odessa, where we rented an apartment in a low-income section of town comprised largely of small, motel-like buildings, dirt streets, and a heavy population of Hispanics. But it was home. Later, we moved to another area of town and into a nice duplex on East 42 Street.

The Welex work schedule was three and three—three weeks of straight work followed by three days off, so every other three-week time segment, we drove ten hours back to Wewoka to spend time with our families. West Texas had terrible dust storms, and there were times when we returned to Odessa in the middle of the night to find our yellow kitchen covered in a layer of red sand from top to bottom. It seeped in through the cracks around the side door that led into the kitchen from the outside and blanketed everything inside with a gritty shroud.

We didn't have air-conditioners, but we did have an evaporative water cooler, which hung out our bedroom window to help keep us comfortable in the hot summer months. But sometimes the temperature was so hot out side, I had to buy a block of ice to cool the water that circulated through the cooler.It made a considerable difference to our comfort inside; but it was temporary, because in that heat, it didn't take long for the ice to melt. Life in West Texas proved to be a test of endurance.

But this experience taught me that our attempts to avoid the storms in life can and often will create more agony. Sometimes it is better to face the storm and go through it, and trust that you'll be okay—even if it's a bit hot and dust-covered—when you do reach the other side.

Thou therefore endure hardness, as a good soldier of Jesus Christ. (II Timothy 2:3 KJV)

CHAPTER FOURTEEN

RESIN QUALITY

A resin is used in the manufacturing process of varnishes and paint. It is added to improve both the quality and the usability of the substance, and the same principle applies to each of our lives with character. Throughout our lives, there are moments and situations that come along—or get "added" to us, if you will—that shape our character for better or for worse, based on how we respond to them. They are character resin.

One weekend on a rare day off from Welex, I drove over to New Mexico with my buddy, Doyle Cook, to check out a new job. I was ready to part ways with life in West Texas, and Doyle thought I might get a job with BJ, another oil-field service company, where he worked. But my impromptu road trip made Dorothy so mad, she called her parents and told them she was through with me and ready to move home. They said, "You're not coming home. You married him and you can stay with him." It saved our marriage.

I didn't get the job anyway.

CHOOSE TO DO THE RIGHT THING BECAUSE IT'S RIGHT

Back in Odessa, I was on twenty-four hour call, which meant if I was needed, I had to go into work, regardless of the hour. One day before dawn, I got called in around five o'clock and stumbled into the shop, my eyelids at half-mast and a chip on my shoulder. My boss, Floyd Jones, a small but tough man, said, "Cox, you're one of the sorriest SOBs I've ever seen!"

Whipped by his words, I withered inside as he raved and ranted at me for the next five minutes. My chin trembled and dropped to my chest as tears flooded my eyes. Embarrassed and ashamed, I turned and slowly walked into the locker room to change into my work clothes.

In the locker room, I weighed my options. I could go back out and whip Floyd, but that would be sure to get me fired, or I could go back out and make him a good hand. If I got fired, what would I tell Dorothy, and where would I get another job? I thought of Kent, now one year old, and after considerable thought, decided to go back out and make amends with Floyd. I said, "Floyd, if you'll give me another chance, I'll change my ways, and work to make you a good hand." And I set out to do just that.

Fourteen years later, Dorothy and I happened to be in Midland, Texas, so I drove over to Odessa and looked up Floyd. A surprised look came over his face when he saw me. I told him I had started my own paint company and thanked him for his contribution to my life, which helped make a responsible worker out of me. He seemed genuinely glad to see me, and I was glad I had taken the time to express my gratitude for his tough-handed approach with me so many years ago.

Years after that experience, I ran across the following quote that I want to pass on. "Character is developed by facing decisions at first little ones, then larger and larger ones—and choosing what's right until it becomes second nature.

"It's not the big moments that define our character, it's the small ones."

It's tried and tested through many circumstances and the most challenging times. We have to know what is right, and we have to choose to do it." (This excerpt is from the October eighth

72

entry in Tony Dungy's devotional, *The One Year Uncommon Life Daily Challenge*).

It's not the big moments that define our character—it's the small ones. For me, one of those moments happened before an early morning shift and became a different type of wake-up call. Dorothy and I have both had life-changing decisions to make, and they don't often come in brief moments. I've found that momentum is made up of moments, and God defines character as doing right as He defines right, regardless of the cost. The Word of God—the Bible—has defined for me what is right and wrong. Throughout all the dilemmas and decisions I faced, the Word of God has shown me the way through. It has lit my path and led me in the right way.

For the commandment is a lamp, and the teaching is light; and reproofs for discipline are the way of life.
(Proverbs 6:23)

CHAPTER FIFTEEN

SUCCESS COMES IN SHADES

In August 1960, while we still lived in Odessa, we drove up to Oklahoma to visit our folks. That's when my parents told me about a paint salesman that used to come through Wewoka who had started a paint manufacturing company in Oklahoma City. His name was Carl Ballew, and he and his partner, Bill Smith, co-owned Capitol Paint, located in an area of the city called Capitol Hill. I drove over to talk with him and though I knew little about the paint business, he hired me for $1.35 per hour, but with no paid overtime. My salary at Welex was a $1.75 per hour and with overtime it averaged $220 per week. Capitol's offer was a good deal less, but I agreed to take the cut in pay in order to get back to Oklahoma City.

LESS LEADS TO MORE

We returned to Odessa where I quit my job with Welex, rented a U-Haul trailer and loaded it with our pink washing machine, TV, baby bed and the rest of our things. And with that, we headed back to Oklahoma. Six to eight months prior to the job change, I had traded my '54 Oldsmobile in for a new white '60 Oldsmobile 88, which came with payments and a little bit of hail damage. This car looked like it was carved out of a flat block of icc by an uninterested Cub Scout, but I still loved all those long, straight lines that ended in hints of the Oldsmobile's fin-heavy past.

Like many other employees, I worked forty-five hours per week at Capitol Paint with no overtime, but when one of the guys quit and reported this practice to the labor commission, the company was ordered to pay us overtime as well as our back pay. But the company found a way around the commission's decision. Their ultimatum . . . sign our checks back to them or get fired. We all needed a job, so we signed our checks back to the company.

After I had worked about six months, Bill promoted me to the position of Plant Manager. One day he said, "Joe, if you work hard, some day you'll make $10,000 a year and will be able to send your kids to college." I never dreamed I would ever make that much money, because my income at the time was about $3,000 a year.

Paint samples are printed on cards that show the various shades of a particular color, with the shades transitioning from light to dark. Often success comes that way, in incremental transitions instead of all at once. Success at one level leads to the next level, and each season of success gets more intense.

Bill Smith took me under his wing, taught me a trade, and I will be forever grateful to him for that. While at Capitol Paint: I ran the plant, made lab batches, and was in charge

> **"Success at one level leads to the next level and each season of success gets more intense."**

of quality control for all the paints. I did not consider myself to be real smart, but I was teachable. Bill was an ex-marine and meaner than a junkyard dog. He demanded a neat workshop, and didn't want to have to repeat himself twice. I didn't want to be yelled at so I worked hard to please him. Like Floyd Jones, my former boss at Welex in Odessa, Bill made a man out of me and in the process, taught me good work habits.

SETBACKS ARE SETUPS FOR SUCCESS

In September, we moved into a duplex in Oklahoma City owned by a couple we called, "Mr. and Mrs. Bryan," who occupied the other side. Dorothy was hired by Cities Service Gas Company to work in the record department, and their offices were in the First National Bank building downtown. When possible, she rode to work with some acquaintances of ours, Preston and Shirley Clark; otherwise, she rode the bus.

Our finances were tight one day, so she was forced to prevail upon the Clarks for a quarter to pay her bus fare, a simple request that nevertheless was extremely difficult for her to make. Sometimes you have to take a step back in order to move forward, and often the greatest promotions initially look like setbacks.

The small unit we called home had a front room, dining room, bedroom, bathroom, and kitchen. Our typical evening meal consisted of: chicken-fried steak, fried potatoes, green beans and gravy, all loaded with ingredients that we had grown up on and tasted delicious. But while we loved all those southern style dishes, they elevated our cholesterol, unbeknownst to us at the time.

We enrolled Kent in the Crestwood Baptist Church Day Care, with its convenient location just down the street from our home. The daycare center forwarded our name to the church secretary, who in turn called and invited us to attend their Sunday morning services.

Maybe it was my new career or the pressures of being a new husband and father, but I had a newfound willingness and curiosity about God. God won't force us to follow Him; He gives us the gift of choice. The decision is ours: God speaks, He leads, He guides, He will even show us His plan and dream, but we have to make the choice to follow. It took a while to get there, but I was finally at the place in my life where I wanted to learn and to stay teachable.

A poor, yet wise lad is better than an old and foolish king who no longer knows how to receive instruction.

(Ecclesiastes 4:13)

CHAPTER SIXTEEN

TESTING THE WATER

At this time, revivals were not even a blimp on my radar let alone a common occurrence in my life. But one night, a flashy dresser named Angel Martinez preached one at Crestwood Baptist Church, so Dorothy and I went. Without knowledge of my turbulent, rebellious, troublemaker past, during the invitation, he made it a point to walk back to where I was seated and ask me to come to the altar.

I wasn't embarrassed, but figured he could see the spiritual darkness etched on my countenance. I liked to drink alcohol and smoke cigarettes. Habits picked up in junior high school that had long been a part of me; and although I knew it was wrong, it was still a big part of my life. Out of guilt and not conviction, I walked down the aisle of that church and was baptized the next Sunday night.

That act of contrition had little affect on my life, because it failed to bring about the changes I desperately needed (but didn't yet recognize). Decisions made out of guilt often fail to last, because they lack genuine repentance and sincerity.

The Sunday School class we attended focused an inordinate amount of time on the perils of alcohol and cigarettes and the need to tithe, which I wanted no part of. The lessons made me feel guilty, because I liked to drink and smoke: in fact, they were a major part of my identity. My habits defined who I was, and I was comfortable with my life as a drinker and smoker. But all the while, in the background of my mind lurked this incessant awareness they were wrong, and it haunted me.

WHAT ARE YOU PLANTING IN YOUR LIFE?

In 1963, we built a new three-bedroom house on NW 104 Terrace, priced at $14,000. I painted it myself to cover the cost of the down payment. We installed a stockade fence and thought we were rich. That spring our yard needed grass; so instead of buying sod, we drove along the road that skirts Lake Hefner, dug up the groundcover we found there, and planted it in our front yard. One day my boss dropped by, pointed at the lawn, and said, " Why did you plant all that chickweed? Haven't you heard of grass?"

We pulled it up and started over. The neighbors must have thought we were nuts.

And just like that chickweed, whose root system is shallow and easily pulled up, my life choices led to weeds in my yard and weeds in my life.

To afford the house, I had to sell our '60 Oldsmobile. We traded it for a '63 Buick, the forerunner of today's sensible sedans, and a '54 Pontiac, which was essentially an upended canoe on wheels. They were both green, they were both two-doors, and, best of all, we owned both of them free and clear, which eliminated our car payment.

Capitol Paint was located on SW 23 Street and we lived on NW 104 Street—a considerable distance apart. Much to my chagrin, that Buick was addicted to oil and every two days on my way home from work, I had to stop at the Knox station and buy two quarts of bulk motor oil at ten cents a quart to feed its habit.

> "Now that I think about it, that car and I both had addictive behavior problems. It was a drinker and a smoker just like me."

Now that I think about it, that car and I both had addictive behavior problems. I drank two quarts of beer and my car drank two quarts of oil. It was a drinker and a smoker just like me

Do you struggle with a destructive habit? Do you make excuses for why you have become the type of person that you are? You won't change unless you get intentional about it, because a new direction always requires a new decision.

When I realized the habits and lifestyle I had adopted led to no good end, I made a new choice. Self pity delays change. The focus of our faith means we must do whatever is necessary to line up with Gods call for our life. And every one has a call on their life. To get your life headed in a new direction, you have to be bold enough to admit it and honest enough to make a change. It isn't often easy, but don't be mistaken, it is well worth it.

The highway of the upright is to depart from evil; he who watches his way preserves his life.   (Proverbs 16:17)

CHAPTER SEVENTEEN

ADDING TO THE MIX

On May 29, 1963, Dorothy gave birth to our second son, Kirk, at St. Anthony Hospital in Oklahoma City. Unlike Kent, Kirk was born completely bald, but what he lacked in hair he made up for in strength of will and stubbornness. Potty training him came down to a battle of the wills. When Dorothy took his diaper off, and set him on the potty chair, he cried and waited. When she gave in to his cries, removed him from the potty chair, and re-diapered him, he proceeded to do his business.

He sucked his thumb, and carried a blanket around with him, which he later exchanged for his training pants. The kids in the neighborhood referred to Kirk as "the underwear kid." When he was six, he sucked his thumb. One day I said to him, "Kirk, if you will stop sucking your thumb, and give up the training pants, I'll buy you a bike with training wheels." He stopped immediately. The strong will I saw in Kirk was a reflection of myself. I always felt I was in a battle between who I was and who others wanted me to be.

KNOW YOURSELF

After three-plus years in the paint business, I decided enough was enough. It was a dirty job and I wanted a career that had a different dress code. Years earlier, when we were in Odessa, I had purchased a policy from Southwestern Life Insurance Company. It required a change in dress, so I thought I'd try my hand at insurance sales. Earl Newton, their branch manager in Oklahoma City, met with me and afterward sent me to Dallas to learn product knowledge. I joined the church near our house up north, not to get the much-needed spiritual nourishment my life needed, but to build a prospective client list.

A short time later, my company hired a new sales manager from East Texas. It didn't take long for me to see that this new boss liked to party and chase women way more than he liked to work. Our work took place in the evenings when people were generally at home, but we spent more time in bars than in homes.

After eighteen months, the consequences of our work habits began to show. Our water, gas, and electricity were turned off, and we got behind in our house payments. My folks mailed us enough money to get the utilities turned back on. My wardrobe change in order to sell something wasn't what I had hoped it would be. Instead, it added stress to our already strained marriage and family. I lived for myself, and in the meantime, my marriage plummeted.

I had become the source of my problems. Blind to the consequences my choices brought, they caught up not only with me, but also with my family. No one gets rid of his problems, which are buried deep inside. You can't run from what is in you. Focus, not on what you've lost, but look at what you have left, and admit your mistakes. Let God help you move forward.

The prudent sees the evil and hides himself, but the naïve go on, and are punished for it. (Proverbs 22:3)

CHAPTER EIGHTEEN

A LIFE OF CONTRAST

Our financial situation worsened until the bank foreclosed on our home and sent us down the road. I made arrangements with a guy I knew to move our stuff back to Wewoka, where Dorothy and the kids moved in with her father, Wayne. Her parents had divorced six years earlier and he lived alone.

Humbled and humiliated by this experience, both of us were so embarrassed and ashamed, we disappeared under the cover of night without a word to our friends. My repeated job failures and our many moves back and forth proved to be more than Dorothy could take. On top of that, she was pregnant with our third child.

We lived in a pressure cooker. The care required by Kent and Kirk combined with our destitute financial situation made us feel like the lid was about to blow. Our marriage was more fragile and precarious than ever before, and neither of us was sure of what would happen next.

THERE IS LIGHT IN THE DARK

In desperation Dorothy called out to God, and He told her clearly, "Don't worry, I will take care of you." Those words were like manna to her soul, and for the next few months, she lived on that promise. God's promise of provision infused her with hope for a brighter tomorrow and drew her to Himself.

One night, Dorothy dreamed she was on a dark path that led through a forest; but at the end of the path was a bright light, and in her dream, she knew that once she reached the light, she would be all right. In reflection, she now knows that the light she saw represented Jesus Christ. "I am the light of the world; he who follows Me will not walk in darkness, but will have the light of Life" (John 8:12).

Whatever God brings you to, He will bring you through.

James Buchanan, my brother-in-law, lived in Dallas and worked for an insurance company. Aware of our circumstances, he sent me to Roswell, New Mexico to sell insurance to the local farmers. I was twenty-six and wrecked my car the first week I was there. After two months, I returned to Wewoka for the weekend. My second venture into the insurance field had come to a dismal end, and once again, I felt like a failure.

While there, Dorothy began to go into labor. Wewoka had a hospital, but I chose to take her to the hospital in Holdenville, and May 23, 1965, she gave birth to our third son, Tony. He was a beautiful baby with an easy disposition and a head full of blonde hair.

Not long after he was born, we took the children, along with our furniture and other household goods, and moved into an apartment in Irving, Texas. There I found work in a machine shop, and operated a mill from four o'clock in the afternoon to midnight, six days a week. The repeated failures of the past hung over us like a dismal, dark cloud that haunted us with memories that worked to convince us that we would never make it to the light. We had lost our house, we had no money, and my sister and brother-in-law helped keep groceries in our cupboard. Our spirits were about as low as a couple's could get.

THERE IS HOPE IN DESPAIR

Dorothy found a job as a receptionist with Frito-Lay, and we hired a middle-aged, red haired, full-bosomed woman to keep the boys. Kent was in the second grade, Kirk was two years old, and Tony was two months. We needed a sitter, but this woman's hygiene was almost more than I could take. When she heated

Tony's food, she stuck her finger in it to check the temperature. Then she licked her finger and scratched her head. The sight of that about killed me. She boasted about going to the dance hall on the weekends, but I couldn't believe anyone would ever dance with her.

One night, our despair and remorse was more than we could bear and as we talked, our past failures, tumbled out between us. We talked about my choppy work history: our constant relocations back and forth, our marriage in shambles, past mistakes, three kids, dependent on handouts, and no money, all of which combined to paint a vivid picture of dismal failure. All the while I was looking for a better job, but believed that prospective employers were turned off by the hopelessness they saw on my face.

Even though I had the vision, the darkness overwhelmed the hope I clung to, and our conversation grew blacker and blacker. Convinced we were a burden to every one, we planned to turn on the gas stove in the kitchen before we went to bed, lay down, go to sleep, and just never wake up. Thank God we couldn't bring ourselves to follow through.

At the time, we saw our life together from the perspective of dread. Our outlook was full of pressure, doubt, and worry—the negative spectrum. But even in the darkest of times, there is a hope to hold on to, even if you have to fight for it.

Hope in God helped us trust and believe the best about the days to come. I love Psalm 42, because the writer refused to give up when assaulted with hopelessness. He knew how to overcome the attack, so hold on to hope, persevere, and don't give up.

Why art thou cast down, O my soul? And why art thou disquieted within me? Hope thou in God: for I shall yet praise Him, who is the health of my countenance, and my God. (Psalm 42:11 KJV)

CHAPTER NINETEEN

PAINTING A NEW PICTURE

Homesick, both Dorothy and I were desperate to move back to Oklahoma City. I called a friend, Oren Childers, who had started a company called Del Paint in Del City (a suburb of Oklahoma City), and told him I needed a job. He said, "Joe, come on back, you've got a job with us." The light was still out there, and so was the glimmer of hope.

Dorothy holding Tony with Kirk outside the Delwood Apartments in 1966.

I took Dorothy and our three boys back to Wewoka, and borrowed Dad's boring but functional, blue, three-quarter-ton pickup truck. With its hefty, five-speed stick shift, guttural-growl-motor, and singular wide bench seat, my brother, Johnny, and I drove to Irving and rented a U-Haul trailer. We loaded our furniture and delivered it to Delwood Apartments at I-40 and Scott Street in Del City, unloaded it, and then drove back to Irving for the rest of our belongings and made the return trip to Del City.

The combination of the long and lengthy road-trip, which totaled 600 miles, the arduous effort to load and unload our stuff, plus the brief time we had to complete the move made for a grueling day's work. Exhausted and worn out, but still determined to turn things around, I made it to work the next morning for my first day on the job at Del Paint.

Delwood Apartment complex was the armpit of Oklahoma County. Hopelessness, despair and depression hung over that place like a black cloud. It seemed like someone committed suicide there at least once a week; not the best environment to try to shake off our own black thoughts, but it was all we could afford.

My job with Del Paint lasted about six months, when my old mentor, Bill Smith, the chemist at Capitol Paint, offered me a job. His latest venture was a company called Gemini Lacquers and to get me to change jobs, he offered me a higher salary than I currently earned. Even though it was a small place located out on North Council Road, I leapt at the opportunity to join him once again.

Strapped financially, our Thanksgiving meal that year was peanut butter and jelly sandwiches. For Christmas, my brother, Jim, sent us a thirty-dollar check to buy the boys Christmas presents. We bought each of them a toy Texaco gasoline truck, then returned to the apartment, wrapped them, and nestled the packaged toys under the tree. Our excited boys waited with baited breath to open those trucks that Christmas morning, and played with them until they were exhausted.

Now that I think back on it, those trucks were a symbol of a long journey that was to come. One life lesson I have learned is that work itself has its reward—

"If you keep your faith in God and continue to work, the reward will come."

if you will pay the price, you will likely succeed, but that success requires diligence. Rewards aren't earned because something gets started, and there are no rewards when you quit, but if you keep your faith in God and continue to work, the reward will come. It's like those gasoline trucks; you have to be in it for the long haul.

I believe many people are unhappy, because they want what comes easy and is convenient. That saddens me, because when people have that mentality, they wind up as losers. They cheat themselves out of the good life God has for them. Don't allow discouragement to seep in. You have to be diligent and do the difficult aspects inherent in any project, if you're ever to succeed. I write this to remind you that I didn't experience overnight success.

For many years, I worked hard and saw little results. In actuality, I had made progress, but there were so many things in my life that needed to be fixed, I was blind to the good changes that had happened along the way; they were there, I just didn't see them. Cling to the fact that God is always at work and His work is always good.

It just might take some time for you to see it.

And let us not lose heart in doing good, for in due time we shall reap if we do not grow weary.

(Galatians 6:9)

CHAPTER TWENTY

RUMBLINGS OF SPIRITUAL CHANGE

One Saturday, a few weeks after we moved into Delwood Apartments, Pastor John Bisagno from Del City's First Southern Baptist Church knocked on our door, introduced himself, and invited us to church. We told him straight out, "We're mad at God! We've lost our house and have a mountain of problems!"

That didn't deter him in the least, because his Saturday visits continued, and during one of his visits Brother John said, "If you'll come to church tomorrow, my wife and I will take you and your family to Alamo Plaza Chicken Restaurant on South Robinson for lunch."

Well, that sounded too good to be true, but before he left, he managed to convince me. I said, "We'll be there." Truth be known, I didn't believe he would remember us, or his offer to take us to lunch. I was wrong. The next day, we attended church, went forward at the end, and moved our membership letter from Village Baptist Church to First Southern Del City Baptist Church.

True to his word, Brother John took us to lunch and we began to attend his church on a regular basis. But once again, I did not agree with the topic of study in our Sunday School class, because it zeroed in on the destructive vices of alcohol and cigarettes. It seemed to me that every Sunday they majored on my vices.

YOU CAN'T CONQUER
WHAT YOU WON'T CONFRONT

The Sunday School teacher wasn't the only one concerned with the issue of my drinking—it was also a deep concern to Dorothy. So, one day when I came home from work, she took me to see Brother John. She must have been at her wits end, because when we walked into his office, she blurted out, "Joe has a drinking problem."

Shocked, my face must have turned ten shades of red, but she was on a roll and didn't stop there!

"He goes to the bars after work and comes home late."

Cornered and in a complete state of shock and disbelief, I felt naked and exposed, because this was the first time my penchant for alcohol had been so blatantly laid bare and in front of the preacher at that.

Brother John could see the shock on my face and struck while the iron was hot taking up right where Dorothy left off. He said, "Joe, you drink because it gives you courage to say what you want to say and do what you want to do. If you have the Holy Spirit living inside you, He will give you courage to face your problems and you won't need alcohol."

Thank God, He's persistent and never gives up on us. Every day we should lift up our life and say, "Holy Spirit, you are welcome here."

I made no commitment to change that day, and Brother John realized there was more to the story. The next day he called

> **"Thank God, He's persistent and never gives up on us."**

Dorothy, who had not escaped his keen eye of discernment. God used his call and Brother John's wise counsel to help her realize that she, too, had areas in her own life that needed to be examined. After his call, she began the painful process of self-examination and realized the truth in Brother John's words.

Each of us needed to be willing to confront our past's individual demons and this was the place we had to start.

What needed to be changed was not our circumstances or living conditions or job situations. What needed to be changed was us.

God knows your future: He saw you before you were formed in your mother's womb, He sees you at this very moment, and He also sees the end of your life as well. He knows, that without confidence and faith, you cannot step into the future and confront and deal with the weak and the wavering side of who you are. And until you do, you cannot eliminate the things that hold you back. If you confront the temporary, the results will be temporary. If you confront the eternal, the results will be eternal.

For the one who sows to his own flesh shall from the flesh reap corruption, but the one who sows to the Spirit shall from the Spirit reap eternal life. (Galatians 6:8)

CHAPTER TWENTY-ONE

PAINT BY NUMBERS

Bill Smith's partner convinced him that he should expand his business into Arkansas, and they wanted me to move to Ft. Smith to open the new plant. The first week I worked at Gemini, my creditors found me and threatened to garnish my wages; a situation which sorely displeased Bill. Thank God someone gave me the good advice to contact Retail Credit Services.

Dorothy and I scheduled an appointment and were instructed to bring all our bills with us to the session. They prorated our salaries to pay off our debts and contacted everyone we owed and arranged to pay our creditors. I didn't have a clue as to how much money we owed. At the time Dorothy worked for an insurance company to help supplement our income, but it wasn't enough to make a dent in our bills. We were underwater in debt and knew, however painful it might be, financial adjustments had to be made.

While I had the social morals of an alley cat, I did have three deep, long-held beliefs, three courses of action that I strongly

> **"It's important to learn the financial habit of working, giving, saving, and then spending."**

believed were not options: abortion, bankruptcy, and divorce. None of those were on the table.

It's important to learn the financial habit of working, giving, saving, and then spending. When you learn these habits, and put them into practice, you will find that God will increase your financial ability. And then, as you make more, you will be able to give more, save more, and spend more. Make an extra payment on a loan instead of another purchase. It can make a huge difference. You can be debt-free, if you want to be, so pray about it and ask God to help you.

Do not be among those who give pledges, among those who become sureties for debts. If you have nothing with which to pay, why should he take your bed from under you? (Proverbs 22:26-27)

SENSE ABOUT DOLLARS

Our agreement with Retail Credit Services required us to endorse our paychecks over to them, and they in turn gave us enough money to survive on. In addition, we signed an agreement in which we promised we would not make another purchase on credit for at least the next four years.

I painted apartments for extra work at night and on Saturdays, which paid $30 a unit. We applied that toward our rent and when that was met, we had a little extra money to spend. This was the first time I had ever been held accountable, and thanks to the strict guidelines of Retail Credit Services, we paid off all our debt and learned valuable financial lessons in the process.

The business in Arkansas failed to develop, so my job with Gemini lasted a month at best, which once again put me on the street in need of a job. Thankfully, my friend Oren Childers at Del Paint rehired me.

One Saturday, Dorothy and I were out for a drive and passed a house on Vickie Drive in Del City with a sign in the yard that read, "For Sale by Owner." I parked the car along the curb, went up to the house, and knocked on the door. They wanted $200 for their equity, so our friends, Joan and Harry Currie, loaned us the money and we moved in. I worked at Time Freight Lines on Saturday to repay Harry and did so until the debt was paid in full.

LISTEN TO THE VOICE OF REASON

A chance encounter at a paint club meeting one night brought Bill Smith back across my path. Once again he offered me a job with Gemini Lacquers, but this time he sweetened his offer with a higher salary, plus a car. That caught my attention. The news upset Dorothy, because the last job with Gemini had been short-lived. But the lure of the added perks enticed me, so in spite of her objections, I took the job anyway.

Bill received assistance from the El Reno Industrial Authority, so he agreed to build a new plant in nearby El Reno. He promoted me to Vice President of Production—my first big title, and it came with my own office. The business in Oklahoma was in the midst of expansion and enjoyed a lucrative time, but I lived in Del City, which made for a sixty-mile daily commute and a long day.

For those of us who worked at the new Gemini plant in El Reno, it didn't take long to for us to locate the bars in our new town. And after work: we picked out a bar, made a beeline straight to it, shot pool, and drank beer for at least two or three hours. By the time I made it home, it was well after 11 o'clock. My old habits dogged me and managed to find a way to resurface.

One night, Dorothy was so mad, she locked me out of the house and left my packed bags parked on the front porch, so I slept in the car. The next day I promised her I would never do it again—a promise I knew was destined to be broken. The only reason we didn't divorce is because: we had three children, nowhere to go, no place to stay, and no money. We were hemmed in.

Sometimes not having money can be a good thing.

I discovered that you can't drink your sorrows away, because every time I tried to drown them, I found that all my sorrows could swim.

Wine is a mocker, strong drink is raging; and whosoever is deceived thereby is not wise.   (Proverbs 20:1 KJV)

CHAPTER TWENTY-TWO

WHITEWASHED

Whitewash is not a term exclusive to painting—it also has a deeper meaning as in the use of deceptive words or actions to disguise faults and errors. Whitewash is a way to cover up a problem. Efforts to whitewash something end in a total loss.

In 1971, Carl Ballew called me and said, "Joe, I want to sell Capitol Paint, and I have a plan to help you purchase it." I had no money for such a venture and told him so, but his plan involved a salary and bonuses. He assured me it would be more than adequate to buy the business.

Convinced, I left Gemini and went to Capitol, but my first day there, I knew I had made a mistake.

The first problem emerged when I noticed that, without the presence of his secretary, Carl would never speak with me. She was the one who ran the company, not him. He was too involved in local politics and didn't have time for his business: and I did not want a woman for a boss. I had always done my own thing—and now I had a woman telling me what to do. It was too much to swallow. I didn't like the change and while his plan sounded good, I doubted I would ever own the company.

Depressed and angry with myself for leaving Gemini, combined with dissatisfaction in the workplace, fueled my desire to drink even more, which I did. When a person has a problem with alcohol and other problems in their life develop, alcohol becomes a way of escape.

I knew that I was trying to whitewash my problems with alcohol. To have a new life, I knew I hat to quit hiding behind it; I had come to the place where I was willing to know and live out the word of God. That meant alcohol had to go. The Bible contains the directions we need to live our lives by, but I needed to learn how to implement those directions. If we ignore it, we live without a sense of fulfillment. If we follow it, we will find the life God has for us.

"To have a new life, I had to quit hiding."

He is on the path of life who heeds instruction, but he who forsakes reproof goes astray. (Proverbs 10:17)

CHAPTER TWENTY-THREE

LET GOD HOLD THE BRUSH

One day in April I came home from work and sat down at the table to eat the dinner Dorothy had prepared, but she didn't eat. The next two nights were a repeat of the night before. On the fourth night, I said, "The past four nights, you have not eaten dinner with me, and I want to know why."

She handed me an article from Guideposts magazine about a woman who had prayed and fasted that God would deliver her husband from alcohol and He did. I read it, threw it on the floor and said, "I don't have a problem with alcohol, and I don't care if you starve to death!"

DON'T BE AFRAID TO ADMIT
HOW THINGS REALLY ARE

Ten days later I was in a bar—appropriately named The Forget-It Lounge, located two blocks west of Capitol Paint in Oklahoma City—drinking beer for lunch. Over the past ten months, I had spent more than a fair amount of time in that pit, a rough place so filled with smoke a person couldn't see the one in front of him, after he walked through the front door.

The putrid stench of foul body odor combined with cheap booze and stale cigarettes was strong enough to gag a maggot, but I didn't care; I just wanted to drink my beer. When a person's depressed and his life's in shambles, the stranger on the nearest bar stool, willing to listen to your knapsack full of problems, becomes a friend. And for me, friendship's common denominator was alcohol.

So there I was, a few days after Dorothy had fasted and prayed that I would be delivered from alcohol, sitting in the Forget-It Lounge drinking a liquid lunch. Seated on that bar stool, I mulled over the myriad of bad decisions made over my lifetime. Behind the smelly, smoke-filled bar hung a big mirror so grimy you could write your name on it. As I looked at myself in the dingy thing, I pondered my equally dingy past, and didn't like what I saw—a thirty-two-year-old man who had a wonderful wife and three wonderful sons, but whose life was headed nowhere but down.

January 1972 - My old look. I lost the smile.

If you are frustrated with your life, maybe it's because your efforts to manage it don't include God. The average paintbrush is made up of a bunch of fibers bound to a handle with a metal ferrule, and costs about $14.85. The brush is nothing special, but in the right hand, it can create something priceless.

A master painter can take a cheap, common, everyday object and transform it, through a few strokes of color, into a work of great beauty and value. The same is true for our life. When placed in the hand of God, our ordinary life is transformed into a life of great worth. But each of us has to decide if we will let go and allow God to hold the brush.

He who loves pleasure will become a poor man; he who loves wine and oil will not become rich.

(Proverbs 21:17)

As I sat on that barstool in that cheap dive, I mulled over these things, and something utterly amazing happened: God spoke to me as clear as day. He said, "Joe, I'm tired of putting up with you. You change or I'm going to take your life."

In that instant, I thought of Grandma Cox, who had prayed for me as a child. She had died two years earlier at the age of ninety-seven, but I remembered her prayers and recalled her oft-repeated words: "Someday, you will serve God."

My canned reply to her at the time had been an insincere, "Thanks, Grandma," followed by a patronizing little pat on the top of her head, thinking all the while, *Yeah, that's the last thing I am ever going to do.*

SAY YES TO JESUS

I also thought about Dorothy, who loved me and wanted me to change, and of the poor example I was setting for my boys Kent, Kirk, and Tony. I got off the bar stool, drove to our house on Vickie Drive, and told Dorothy what God had said to me. There by our bed, I got down on my knees and, and with my heart filled with genuine repentance, I asked God to save me, forgive me of my sins, and deliver me from alcohol.

When I stood up, I was a new person.

The hold alcohol had on me was gone. Instantly. It was as if the heavy weight draped around my shoulders was lifted. I was suddenly and miraculously set free, like a bird held captive whose prison bars were opened and set free to soar into the heavens. Hope flooded my heart and unspeakable joy filled my soul. The grass was greener, the sky was bluer, and the sun shined brightly on a new day. And it was indeed a new day.

Because he hath set his love upon me, therefore will I deliver him; I will set him on high, because he hath known my name. (Psalm 91:14 KJV)

KNOW JESUS, KNOW CHANGE

I asked Dorothy to follow me back to work where I walked into the office, handed Carl my keys, and said, "I quit," and turned to leave.

Disbelief and a deer-in-the-headlights look spread across his face as he said, "But Joe, what are you going to do for a job?"

"I don't know, Carl, but I do know that I'm going to live for the Lord."

He laughed and shook his head. He knew me well and doubted my newfound peace with God was real.

But it was real—God had changed me and delivered me from alcohol. He made me a new person. And with the Lord's help, I have never had a drink of alcohol since that day.

Therefore if any man is in Christ, he is a new creature; the old things passed away; behold, new things have come.
(II Corinthians 5:17)

The Holy Spirit now lives inside of me, just as Brother John Bisagno said the day Dorothy and I went to talk with him.

Over the next month, Dorothy observed many changes in me, and concluded I was indeed a different person. She saw a peace in my life that she didn't have.

[Joshua said:] And if it seem evil unto you to serve the LORD, choose you this day whom you will serve: ... but as for me and my house, we will serve the LORD.
(Joshua 24:15 KJV)

CHAPTER TWENTY-FOUR

DOROTHY'S BRUSH STROKES:
A WORD FROM DOROTHY

My parents, Wayne and Christine Garret, married at age sixteen and nineteen. They experienced many difficult times, so I often stayed with Grandmother Garrett when I was about five years old. Grandmother and grandfather attended church every Sunday and took me with them.

Grandmother Garrett was an avid Bible reader, and sometimes had me sit with her and listen as she read aloud from the Bible or a story from her Christian magazine. At the time, I did not realize that God would use these times with my grandmother to lay a foundation in my life that He would later build on.

When I was six, we moved to Holdenville, where both sets of my grandparents lived. It was there that I started first grade.

Mother was unfaithful to Dad, and there were marital problems between them. On one occasion Dad said to my sister, Virginia, and me, "Your Mom does not want you so I guess I will have to take you." That was a most difficult and hurtful thing for us to hear, and those hurtful words stayed with us for many years.

Life in a small town meant that everyone knew everyone else's business, so my mother's scandalous affair became common knowledge, which carried with it consequences Virginia and I would have to bare. I was not accepted by many of the other girls in school… except for one nice mother, Mrs. Smith.

NEW HEART, NEW START

I started dating Joe my senior year in high school and we fell in love. He had a strong, stubborn personality, which I admired, and on New Years Eve, he gave me an engagement ring.

After we got married, we experienced many difficult times, which God ultimately used to draw us to Himself. During one season of desperation, I prayed, and poured out my heart to God, and He spoke to me and said, "Don't worry I will take care of you." I lived on that promise, as well as a dream I had which Joe has earlier described.

Soon after that dream, I read Galatians 5:20-21, which states pretty plainly that things like bitterness and anger are in the same category with sin and drunkenness. I looked at Joe's new life and realized he now possessed a peace that I did not have. I finally saw myself as a bitter, angry person without peace in my life.

Shortly after that realization, I read a book called A New Song by Pat Boone, and became aware of the fact that I had never invited Jesus Christ into my heart and life. I had simply joined a church and put my name on their roll, but had never entered into a relationship with the living God in the person of Jesus.

I saw myself, and my sin, and asked Christ to come into my life and forgive me and make me a new person. I realized that all along, He had loved me, when I thought that no one else did.

TRUST

For God so loved the world, that He gave His only begotten Son, that whoever believes in Him, shall not perish but have eternal life. (John 3:16)

PRAY

That if you confess with your mouth Jesus as Lord, and believe in your heart that God raised Him from the dead, you will be saved; for with the heart a person believes, resulting in righteousness and with the mouth he confesses, resulting in salvation... "for WHOEVER will call upon the name of the lord will be saved.

(Romans 10:9-10,13)

BELIEVE

Several years later, my mother came back into my life and went to church with Joe and me. She called Dad, and asked for his forgiveness before he died, and then Joe took care of her until she died.

God is a God of grace and forgiveness. And He is available to each of us when out of our need, we cry out to Him for it. He can make a new person out of the worst sinner. Never forget that there is hope for everyone. Our responsibility is to trust, pray, and believe.

To the Lord our God belong compassion and forgiveness, for we have rebelled against Him; (Daniel 9:9)

CHAPTER TWENTY-FIVE

PRY THE LID OFF

Finally, I had my life in order. I was free from the destructive habits that had plagued me, there was peace in my family, and yet another new career change was on the horizon.

Every year H-I-S sells tens of thousands of cans of paint. Some orders are as small as a single gallon, while others call for a tote, which is two hundred and fifty gallons. However, of all the many different sizes of cans and barrels, they all have one thing in common: lids.

In order to get to the paint, the lid has to be removed. The lid placed on the can forms a seal, which requires prying off if the paint is to be used. Likewise, each person has a lid on his or her life. Think of the word "LID" as an acronym, which stands for Limitations, Inadequacy, and Deficiencies. Every individual has inside of them incredible potential, talent, and ability, but to reach the content within, you must get rid of the LID.

The limitations of our thoughts, the fear of inadequacy and our self-imposed deficiencies have to be removed so that all the talents within us can be released. But how can one remove that lid? Well, sometimes God uses people to pry the lid off, which is exactly what He did in my life.

SOMEONE BELIEVES IN YOU

Harry Currie, who had earlier loaned us $200 for our house, heard I had quit my job at Capitol Paint and remarked to me one day, "Joe, why don't you start a paint company?"

"Well, Harry, I don't have the finances to start a company," I replied.

"You know, Joe, I think you could be successful," he encouraged. "Figure up the costs you'll need and get back with me."

I did what he asked and a few days later returned with the requested information. "I believe I can do it for $10,000 dollars." Harry took me to Del State Bank, where we signed a note for that amount, to be paid off in forty-two months. I had not signed a check since we lost our house in 1965, seven years earlier. Our experience with Retail Credit Services had taught us to live within our means and at this juncture, that experience proved most beneficial as we began this new venture.

WHAT'S IN THE NAME

My sister, Jane, named the company H-I-S Paint. She said, "If you dedicate the company to the Lord, name it H-I-S, so that He gets the credit."

Our first location at 1026 SE 26th. Both of us had lots of hair.

Gerald Gambel Commercial Real Estate Company negotiated a contract on a building located on SE 26 Street, at a rental cost of $400 per month. When the owner of the building learned that this was my first attempt in business, he tried to back out of the deal, but it was too late, the contract had been signed.

The building was a pit, but we made it work for the first three years. We bought: a used, light-blue Chevrolet pickup truck for deliveries, which cost $600, a new mixer machine for $3500, as well as the raw materials I needed to get started. By the last part of May 1972, our first batch of paint was in the mixer.

Rohm and Haas, who at the time was the world's largest manufacturer of acrylic resin, furnished me with a good book of proven product formulas, thanks to their salesmen, Darrell Campbell and Ron Young. The University of Missouri, Rolla also offered courses on Paint Formulating, which I attended three different times. I wanted to learn everything there was to learn about paint.

FIND A WAY TO MAKE IT WORK

Until October 1972, H-I-S Paint had one employee: me. I made the paint, put it in the buckets, labeled them, loaded them onto the truck, and looked for painters to sell it to. Pure acrylic latex, which was

Our first batch ticket.

113

the interior wall paint used for new apartments, sold for $1.95 a gallon. Exterior paint and latex enamel went for $3.30 a gallon. Other paint companies couldn't believe that my paint could be manufactured at such a reasonable price and sent samples of it to their labs. Their test results concluded that it simply could not be done. But it was simple. I could do it because I had no overhead, just me.

From 1972 through the next thirteen years, I focused on latex paint because it was easier to sell. Lacquer was much more expensive. My interior flat latex needed to sell for under $2 a gallon if we were to be competitive in the new apartment market. On Labor Day '72, instead of enjoying a day off, I spent the entire day in the lab making experimental batches of paint in a kitchen blender.

A paint formula is like a cake recipe, in that different products require different ingredients. That day, I added or subtracted different amounts of ingredients and painted samples from each batch on a wall. When I found the one that covered the wall in one coat for under $2 a gallon-selling price, I had a winner. Since then, we have sold hundreds of thousands of gallons of that paint product whose manufacturing costs in today's market has escalated one thousand percent.

During the first couple of years, I cleaned houses at night and on Saturdays for grocery money. When people who lived in the Federal Housing Authority could not meet their house payments and were foreclosed on, they moved out and left the places filthy. I was hired to clean up their messes and make them livable. Work which I was mighty happy to do because it helped make ends meet while H-I-S Paint took hold in the area.

DON'T FEAR HARD WORK

The early stages of H-I-S were tough, and Dorothy was the backbone of my business success. Every morning we prayed together that I would get a new customer. Then she made out a daily call list and at the end of the day, checked to see if I had followed through and contacted everyone on the list. She kept the books for the first two years, sent out statements, paid the bills, and made the payroll. Her constant encouragement was oxygen to my soul. The ant's work ethic described in Proverbs challenged me, and I refused to be a sluggard.

Go to the ant, O sluggard, observe her ways and be wise, which having no chief, officer, or ruler, prepares her food in the summer, and gathers her provision in the harvest. How long will you lie down, O sluggard: When will you arise from your sleep? A little sleep, a little slumber, a little folding of the hands to rest—and your poverty will come in like a vagabond, and your need like an armed man.
(Proverbs 6:6-11)

For some mysterious reason in this time frame, I suffered from unbearable headaches. At times, they were so bad it was difficult to see, but I refused to allow them to keep me from my work. Later, I was blessed to learn that my headaches were caused from an allergy I had developed to chocolate. Once eliminated, the headaches disappeared.

GET INSPIRED

Back when I was in insurance sales, I took a Dale Carnegie course to learn how to sell. As a part of the course, I had to stand in front of the class and say, "If you want to be enthusiastic, you have to act enthusiastic, and boy am I enthusiastic." Before I left for work each day, Dorothy had me stand in front of the mirror and repeat it three times.

Every day we prayed that when we went to the mailbox we would find a check from a customer who had paid his invoice so that we would pay our bills, and God never failed to meet our needs. We lived by faith day-by-day and claimed His promise:

"And my God shall supply all your needs according to His riches in glory in Christ Jesus" (Philippians 4:19). It is the way we have learned to live, and we continue to claim that promise to this day.

WHAT'S YOUR BUCKET?

In the early days of H-I-S, there was an ice-cream company in Oklahoma City that used five-gallon plastic pails for their product. In need of buckets for my own product, I bought those empty pails for ten cents each and had my boys wash off the labels so I could reuse them.

There was a catch, however, in that their product came in different colors. Their white pails had formerly contained chocolate and cherry flavors. Their green pails had contained dill pickles. If we were to convince painters to try our product, we needed to present a uniform package. To accomplish that, we saved the various colored pails until we had accumulated twenty containers of the same color. And with those pails as our paint buckets, we at last began to work on our dream.

Everybody has a bucket. The bucket is the beginning of a dream. Use what you have where you are to get started. It may not seem like much now, but if you won't let discouragement defeat you, your dream will become something great. When you trust God with what you've got, little good things become big good things.

So what's your bucket?

For who has despised the day of small things?

(Zechariah 4:10)

CHAPTER TWENTY-SIX

LIFE-KOTE

Life-Kote is a coating process used to extend the life of outdoor equipment, and it has been a tremendously successful product for H-I-S. Life-Kote has been formulated to withstand tough conditions and is guaranteed to last for the life of the container.

I often think of the spiritual parallel of this product. God made provision for us before the foundations of the world were established. He knew we could not live the life He had planned for us without our acceptance of the free gift of His provision. Just like waste containers or any equipment that is subjected to extreme conditions, without the adequate protective coat He offers, we will deteriorate and our end will be worse than our beginning.

My sister and brother-in-law, Jane and James Buchanan, lived in Wichita, Kansas and were involved in Navigator Bible Studies. When Jane heard about my salvation experience, she encouraged us to join Navigators, a disciple-making organization. She was convinced their home Bible study would be helpful to us as new Christians.

The next Friday night, they came to our house in Del City and brought their friends, Sue and Charles Bankston. George Fooshee, their Navigators' friend in Wichita, told them about a man in Oklahoma City, Gene Warr, who was a strong advocate of Navigators. We looked up Gene's address in the phone book, drove to his house on North McArthur one Saturday night, and knocked on his door. He answered and after he learned the reason for our visit, invited us into his home.

My sister, Jane, told Gene that I was a new Christian and wanted to get into a Navigator home Bible study group. He visited with us for about thirty minutes, during which time I shared my recent salvation experience.

He said, "Invite three or four couples to your home, and in two weeks, I will send a couple to your house." That couple was Jim and Norma Kennedy.

Two weeks later, together with five other couples, we began Book One of the Navigator series. The first night of the study Jim said to me, "Joe, if you and Dorothy want to make it in the Christian walk, you need to read your Bible every day."

He gave me a pamphlet by *Robert Foster called Seven Minutes with God that taught us how to have a quiet time with the Lord through daily Bible reading. He said, "If you don't do this, you will not make it as a Christian." I wanted to change so bad I believed him and followed his advice. *This complete guide is located in the Appendix section.

COVER YOUR LIFE WITH WISDOM

Jim also suggested that I make it a priority to include a chapter from the Book of Proverbs as a part of my daily devotions. He explained that our lives need a road map and without it, they lack direction. Since that time, I've followed his recommendation, and it has helped shape my life. I learned that if I wanted to impact the lives of our employees and the world around them, integrity and ethics must be evident in my personal life as well as my professional life.

> "I learned that if I wanted to impact the lives of our employees... then integrity and ethics must be evident in my personal life as well as my professional life."

Jim pointed out that, since there are thirty-one chapters in the book of Proverbs, I could easily read one chapter for each day of the month, starting over at chapter one every month. Over the course of a year, I will have read the Book of Proverbs twelve times. He also suggested that I read at least one chapter a day from a different book of the Bible, and to start in the New Testament and read through it book by book.

Afterwards, Jim suggested I pray and ask God for His direction and protection for the day, confess my sins and lay my needs before Him. This has become a daily thirty-minute investment that I cannot do without. Since that day, I have never veered from this practice in over forty years. Over the past twenty years, I have read through the entire Bible each year.

That Bible study with Jim and Norma lasted three years and birthed three others. Over the past forty years, I have been blessed to take many new believers through the Navigators Bible study books.

LIVE WHAT YOU BELIEVE

When we returned from Gene's home that night, my sister said, "Joe, there is another thing you need to quit." I knew what she meant· I had developed a nasty habit for cigarettes in seventh grade and held on to ever since. The six of us held hands around our coffee table; I laid my pack of Winston's down, and asked God to take away my desire to smoke. He did and I have never smoked a cigarette since.

Dorothy and I bought two Bibles and read from them every day. God's word teaches us and gives powerful encouragement and strength to face life. It's a book of wisdom that has taught me how to live. The truth I found in the pages of God's word has changed my life and continues to change me day by day, and it will do the same for you if you let it. I consider this excerpt to be my life verse:

Blessed is a man who perseveres under trial; for once he has been approved, he will receive the crown of life which the Lord promised to those who love Him.

(James 1:21)

CHAPTER TWENTY-SEVEN

THE MASTER'S PALETTE

A palette is a thin board that has a hole in one end; the artist places his thumb through this hole to grip the palette as he mixes colors while he paints. From there he is able to mix a variety of colors and vary the shade until he gets the right color for his masterpiece. It's a good word picture to describe God's activity in a person's life. Our lives are His canvas.

Christianity was never intended to be a solo way of life. Ever the Great Economist, God uses each situation, every circumstance, every person who crosses our path, and comes into our lives are His instruments; all there by His design and for His purpose. Some are there but for a season: like ships silently passing in the night whose waves lap the shores, they touch us, and change us, and we are never the same. Over the years, many people have come and gone in mine and Dorothy's lives and the lives of our kids, but each has made eternal spiritual deposits that have blessed us beyond measure. Those listed below are but a few.

BENEFIT FROM THE POSITIVE INFLUENCE OF THE FAITH OF OTHERS

In August '72, Brother John Bisagno, who had become the pastor of First Baptist Church in Houston, Texas, returned to Oklahoma to hold a crusade at the state fairgrounds. It was kids' night and when the altar call was given, Kirk and Tony responded and went forward. (Kent had responded to an earlier invitation given by Brother John, when he was our pastor at First Southern Baptist Church in Del City.)

Afterwards Brother John recognized Dorothy and me, and introduced us to Jimmy Draper, the new Pastor at First Southern Baptist Church in Del City. John urged us to return to First Southern, which we did the next Sunday. Since that time, we have been blessed with the godly leadership of Brother Jimmy Draper, followed by Brother Bailey Smith, and Brother Tom Elliff.

God's ministry through our lives began in '75, when I was ordained as a Deacon at First Southern Baptist Church in Del City. Dorothy and I taught in the student ministry until our boys graduated high school. Afterwards, we taught the young adults class. Later, I taught a men's class and Dorothy taught a ladies' class. Dorothy and I have taught Sunday School for thirty-three years.

In '75, as a participant in the Evangelism Explosion course in Ft. Lauderdale, Florida, I was challenged to live out my Christianity in a real and personal way, and that was where the rubber met the road. It forced me to go beyond my comfort zone and engage strangers with the Gospel of Jesus Christ. The course challenges every person to answer two poignant questions about their lives, which we'll now look at in more detail.

THE TWO QUESTIONS YOU MUST ANSWER

1.) Have you come to a place in your spiritual life where you know for certain that if you were to die today you would go to heaven?

2.) Suppose you were to die tonight and stand before God and He were to say to you, "Why should I let you into heaven?" What would you say?

After we returned from Florida, First Southern Baptist Church implemented the Evangelism Explosion program, and

I was asked to train two people: one man and one woman. On Thursday night, we were given the names and addresses of three people who had visited our church in the past, and my team and I were assigned to pay them a follow-up visit. During the visit, we were to ask them the two questions.

Two of the prospects lived close to the church and the other lived about six miles away. The first two were not at home when we stopped by, but I recognized the name of the third person, a man named Ron Wallace, who had recently moved to Oklahoma City from Kansas City.

TURNPIKE TURNAROUND

To say that Ron was flamboyant was a gross understatement. He wore ostrich-skin boots with flashy, bright-colored, western-style suits and drove a red Mercedes convertible with a license tag that read, "Ron POSITIVE Wallace." He wore cuff links with his starched shirts, gold jewelry, and was as bold as a lion.

I told my trainees that his house was too far away, but the truth behind my hesitancy was that he intimated me and I dreaded the thought of talking to him. The trainees insisted that we make the effort, so we drove to his house.

I knocked on his door, and Ron answered. He invited us to step inside where he introduced us to his wife, Sharron, and their daughter. After some small talk, I asked Ron the two EE questions: Have you come to the place in your spiritual life that you know for certain that if you died tonight, you would go to heaven? And suppose you were to die tonight and God would ask you, "Why should I let you into heaven?" What would you say?

Ron answered, "Yes, I know I would go to heaven because my father's a Pentecostal preacher." My team and I let it go at that.

About two weeks later, Ron called to tell me that on his return trip from Tulsa, God had spoken to him about my two questions. He said he pulled off the turnpike, stopped by the side of the highway, asked Jesus to come into his heart and forgive him for his sins.

The next Sunday, Ron was baptized and joined my Sunday School class. The moral of the story: don't prejudge anyone.

I also served as the Deacon's Chairman at First Southern Baptist Church as well as Chairman of the Personnel Committee. But, my greatest honor came when I was appointed to serve on the Board of Trustees at The Southern Baptist Theological Seminary in Louisville, Kentucky under Dr. Albert Mohler, Jr. Founded in 1859 at Greenville, South Carolina; it is the oldest Baptist seminary in the United States.

During Brother Tom Elliff's tenure, Dorothy and I became close friends with him and his wife, Jeannie. During a joint vacation, Tom told us that he and Jeannie prayed for each other every morning for the events of each other's day, because it helped them to know what was happening in their respective schedules.

Dorothy and I adopted their practice and have continued it for twenty-five years. Prayer connects us to the presence of Jesus and as a result, Dorothy and I have a connection with each other that grows stronger each day.

I am the vine, you are the branches; he who abides in Me, and I in him, he bears much fruit; for apart from Me you can do nothing. (John 15:5)

CHAPTER TWENTY-EIGHT

GET THE GRIND

Think of your favorite color. Mine happens to be blue. No matter what color you like or what surface it's painted on, that color had to go through a process to become that color. Every color of paint is made up of pigments, which are those solid substances that impart color and hide in paint formulations. They are the most expensive compounds found in paint, and their powdered form must be properly ground to give the paint its true color. Otherwise, the result is a gritty, low gloss product, which, because it has not been ground to the required degree, will not cover the surface well.

Proper dispersion and fineness of the powered pigment is a vital part in the manufacturing process of a quality paint product. A Hegman Grind gauge is used to evaluate the particle size to insure that the full development of dispersion and fineness has been reached.

In other words: the finer the grind, the brighter the color.

> **"If you submit to the process, you will come through it with a life full of living color."**

God uses a similar process with us when He allows difficult situations and circumstances to develop in our lives. You might say you feel like you've been put through the grind, because you are. Remember, the finer the grind, the more brilliant the color. If you submit to the process, you will come through it with a life full of living color.

We started H-I-S Paint with a bare minimum of capital and a lean budget. In the first couple of years, without a cushion of extra capital, I painted things for our church. Kent, my oldest son, and I painted our church's Falls Creek Cabin. We also painted the motel, theatre, and many church classrooms.

It was in my heart to bless our church in any way that I could and at the time, it was through painting. I started to tithe without ever hearing a sermon on tithing. If Jesus gets your heart, He should also get your pocketbook, and I have learned over the years that you can't out-give God.

WORK HARD, PRAY HARD

H-I-S got off to a slow start in '72 and '73, due to the fact that raw materials were hard to get. With a shortage of those materials, and our allotment of new materials based on the previous year's sales, we struggled. Many mornings I pulled a trailer to Dallas to pick up a supply of raw materials to restock our depleted inventory.

One day I needed some Natrasol, which is a thickener for paint. I called my supplier in Dallas and was told we had exceeded our allotment, and without this product, my paint would be as runny as water. We prayed for a miracle. A couple of days later, I called our supplier again and placed the same order. This time her reply was just what I needed to hear: "It will ship in two days!"

Then there's titanium dioxide, a pigment ingredient found in anything that is white: toothpaste, makeup, paint, plastic, everything. In '75, I ran out, and the only place it could be found was on the black market at a dollar a pound. The regular price was 25 cents a pound. Everyone in our Bible study prayed for titanium.

The next day, when I went to the bank to get a cashier's check to buy one ton of titanium, I saw a salvage dealer I knew.

The man was a wheeler-dealer and always had something to sell or buy. I asked him, "Do you have any titanium?"

He said, "I bought a load of raw materials the other day from a company who's going out of business."

I said, "Is there any titanium dioxide in the load?"

"I don't know, but follow me and I'll see." He found five bags, as well as five bags of red pigment and forty bags of yellow pigment. I bought all the raw materials he had. Two days later, I traded those five bags of red pigment to an Ink Company in Irving, Texas for forty bags of titanium dioxide. Not long after that, I traded the forty bags of yellow pigment for eighty bags of titanium dioxide. God is good.

GO WHERE THE PEOPLE ARE

Our location on SE 26 Street proved to be less than ideal, but it was where H-I-S began. The traffic flow was nil and none. During our first three years, all of our paint sales came as a result of me going outside the plant in search of potential customers.

April, 1975 - Our new location at 921 SW 29th. $600 per month rent.

No one ever came into the plant. When my three-year lease was up in 1975, we moved to SW 29 Street.

To deter break-ins, I bought a German shepherd and named her Dusty. She was a natural when it came to guarding the property. In fact, the first few mornings I tried to open up, she met me with a deep growl, bared fangs, and refused to let me enter. I had to drive back home, pick up Kirk, and drive back to the store, where his arrival was greeted with great excitement and a tail that wagged like a windshield wiper on high. But Kirk had to be the first one through the door. This routine repeated itself each and every morning until Dusty finally allowed me to be the first through the door.

We never had a problem for the three years we were on 26 Street, until one morning, I opened the shop to discover that Dusty had disappeared. Ever a dog lover, I looked for her for several weeks.

About a month later, an employee called early one morning and said, "Joe, there's a dog under the counter." I rushed to work and when she heard my voice, she scrambled out to greet me. Someone had apparently tied her up, because the hair around her neck was worn off. I took her home, bathed her, and fed her a raw steak. I was so glad to have her back I don't know who was happier, Dusty or me.

KEEP ON WORKING

In 1975, my younger brother, Johnny, needed a job, so I hired him to sell paint at a salary of $500 a month. Our new storefront location on 29 Street gave us the much-needed visibility, and with that public exposure people stopped in and purchased products. At last, we were moving in the right direction.

Johnny turned out to be a natural, and after thirty-seven years with H-I-S, thanks largely to his hard work and effort, we became heavily invested in apartments and property management.

If you refuse to allow difficulties to frustrate, intimidate, or discourage you; if you face a challenge head-on and refuse to give up, like color, which is put to the test, your life will be bright and brilliant. Difficulties will come, but don't allow them to daunt you efforts. Whether it's a relationship that needs to be turned around, a debt that needs to be paid, or a new project you want to get off the ground, you can do it with God in the mix.

And men will say, "Surely there is a reward for the righteous; Surely there is a God who judges on earth!"
(Psalm 58:11)

CHAPTER TWENTY-NINE

TRUE COLORS COME THROUGH

We purchased gas for our delivery vehicles at a Texaco station a couple of blocks from our location on 29 Street, and one day as I signed my ticket I noticed a Playboy magazine on the counter. I hadn't looked at one in years, but I still had a brief desire to find out what the centerfold looked like. There is no doubt that success does not keep temptation away; it's always around and each of us must be prepared to face it.

As I signed the ticket, my writing went off the paper while my mind wandered. I didn't look at the magazine, but I also never bought gas there again. I Corinthians 10:13 KJV came to mind: "No temptation has overtaken you but such is common to man; and God is faithful, who will not allow you to be tempted beyond what you are able, but with the temptation will provide the way of escape also, so that you may be able to endure it."

THE TRUTH ABOUT TEMPTATION

I want to share the truth with you about temptation. We must not diminish its significance, because no temptation is insignificant. Temptation targets everyone, and no one is immune to its attack. When temptation comes, don't get discouraged—you're not alone. Everyone faces it and since others have faced this same temptation and overcome it, so can you.

Where there is an opportunity to give in to temptation, God also gives us the option to get out. To avoid it's trap, you must be aware of the places and people where you're most vulnerable, and make an agreement with yourself that when it appears, you will run away from it.

Over the years, I have faced many temptations in various arenas of life, but what I consider to be the greatest temptation that any person will ever face, is the temptation to quit. We may not recognize its disguise, but the discouragement and thoughts that accompany the urge to quit, are a form of temptation. When you know you're supposed to do something, the moment those thoughts surface, say, "I will not quit, I will not give up, I will finish what God has called me to do." Say it out loud. Your ears need to heat it.

"The greatest temptation any person will ever face is the temptation to quit."

I kept a Navigator Bible packet of Scripture verses on the top of the dashboard in my pick-up, which I read from daily. They've helped me maintain a focused walk with the Lord and experience victory over temptation. Temptation will always be around, so a wise person will be prepared to handle it when it comes their way, usually at our weakest moments. To face it, fight it and overcome it, we need to be strong in our prayer life and have the word of God living in our heart. These disciplines keep us connected to God's strength when we are weak.

Watch and pray, that ye enter not into temptation: the spirit indeed is willing, but the flesh is weak.

(Matthew 26:41 KJV)

CHAPTER THIRTY

PEOPLE ARE THE POINT

One day Curtis Harris, a paint contractor, called in an order for thirty gallons of flat latex wall paint, our acoustic ceiling blend. And he requested it be delivered to Warwick West Apartments next to Baptist Hospital. When I delivered it he commented, "If it doesn't clog up my airless spray rig, I'll buy my paint from you." I prayed all the way back to the shop. That afternoon he called and said, "Joe, I have a problem with the paint." My heart sank, but he continued, "I'm out of it. Bring me one hundred gallons." At that, my heart rate leapt off the chart.

SHOW INTEREST IN OTHERS

Another big contractor, Jim Jackson, was cordial to me, but he just wouldn't buy. I called on him anyway, off and on, for at least a year. I didn't make a pest of myself, but just popped in and out on occasion and always left my card. If he wasn't there, I still left my card. I wanted him to know that I was persistent and still interested in his business.

One day my persistence paid off. He called and said, "Joe, I'm mad at my supplier and have decided to purchase from you."

These two contractors painted most of the apartment buildings in Oklahoma City in the '70s and '80s, and were largely responsible for putting us on the map.

Since summer was our peak sales season, our need for raw materials increased. In August, the hottest month of the year, I ordered a railroad boxcar of fourteen hundred, fifty-pound bags of clay, a pigment used in latex paint. I rented a truck, drove to a railroad track siding on the east side of town, unloaded the boxcar by hand, stacked it in my truck, and drove back to our plant where I unloaded it, and stacked it by hand again.

CREATE A SUPERIOR PRODUCT, HIRE SUPERIOR PEOPLE

In those days, we did not have a forklift and worked without one for the next five years. When we moved to our location on 29 Street, I bought our second mixer and a 3,000-gallon bulk storage tank for our acrylic resin. Prior to this, we stored the liquid resin in fifty-five-gallon drums, so this was indeed a big step up.

Resin is the key ingredient in paint—it's the bonding agent that holds the paint together. The more resin used to make the paint, the more superior the paint. At the time, we were the only company who used one hundred percent acrylic resin.

Our early mixers.

At Capitol Paint, my first job in the paint business, I learned that a batch of paint contains an approximate amount of fifteen different ingredients. To test the endurance of the paint, we made test pints, painted them on fence panels and exposed them to the elements.

At H-I-S, our paint is also tested for quality and endurance as well. In fact, one of our paint products comes with a "Lifetime Guarantee."

Like resin, diligence is the refusal to quit, and the decision to do what's right until you reach your goal. And then continue on to be diligent and to maintain what you have achieved. Diligence requires determination. Determination is the mind-set and diligence is the work that goes with it.

Poor is he who works with a negligent hand, but the hand of the diligent makes rich. (Proverbs 10:4)

CHAPTER THIRTY-ONE

SPECTROPHOTOMETER

Before computers and spectrophotometers came along, the old-fashioned way to custom match another color was to find a similar color on a color chart, use that as your point of reference, and make minor adjustments in it until you reach the desired color.

Today's use of computerized color spectrophotometers, have made this a much simpler process. The desired color is placed under the spectrophotometer's eye and a color reading is taken. The computer then crunches the visible wavelength numbers into a color tint formula. That tint formula contains the amount of various colorants that need to be added to a tint base paint to achieve the desired color. This device provides the exact content of what's needed to mix the color, which results in a successful product.

In the late '70s, H-I-S had grown to the point where we needed to hire an additional employee. So one morning during my quiet-time prayer, I asked God to bring us a young man who was not from Oklahoma City. While my specific prayer request may sound strange, I knew what I wanted, and furthermore, I knew that God already knew the very person I needed.

> **"The struggle with hiring great people is finding one with the right motivation."**

Why did I make this strange request? Because I have found that the key to a great employee begins with a search for someone with the right motivation. There are many out there who are more interested in the title than the task. In the interview process, one of the telltale signs I look for is in the potential employee's first question. If it is, "What are your benefits?" That's an immediate deal-breaker,

LOOK AT THE HEART

Over the years, I have found the best employees tend to come from small rural communities, because their ethics tend to be superior to those who have grown up in the city. They may leave those small towns, but they bring their small-town values with them. They are: not afraid to work, they know the value of a dollar, they are respectful, they are grateful to have a job, they are honest, and therefore, they show up for work on time and seldom call in sick.

The next morning, the phone rang and a young man by the name of Chuck Norfleet introduced himself and asked, "Do you need an employee?"

I said, "Where are you from?"

He replied, "Boise City."

I sensed that he could be the answer to my prayer, so I said, "Come see me." He was a young, skinny, eighteen-year-old, fresh out of high school, and just what I had prayed for. In 1976, he became our fourth employee. Thirty-five years later, Chuck still works for H-I-S Coatings. He is now head of Purchasing, as well as a valuable, dedicated employee, a good friend, and from time to time, a companion on the golf course.

Today, most prospective new hires want a position and not a job. For that reason, I contract new employees for three months, which gives me the opportunity to observe their attitudes, temperament, work ethics and other character qualities, which I deem essential if we are to preserve a positive work environment.

Over my lifetime I have observed many business partnerships, but I have yet to see both partners happy. I find it hard to see two equals.

My first opportunity to observe a partnership occurred at my first job with a paint company. One partner handled sales and finances, and the other partner served as the chemist and plant manager. The plant manager thought he carried the major workload, while the salesman thought he contributed the most to the company, because he brought in all the business.

Conflict between the two men continued to escalate, and within four years their partnership had ended. Both men hooked up with other partners later on, but those partnerships failed as well.

When I started my company, among the contractors who bought from us were those who were in partnerships. And over the past forty years, I still have not seen one business partnership that lasted. Beyond that, a good ninety percent of the time we lost money on the account, because when the partnerships dissolved, each partner told us the other partner was responsible to pay the bill.

There are surely partnerships that have been a success somewhere, but I have never witnessed one in person; it is much easier to get into a partnership than it is to get out of one.

God does not look for successful people to make faithful, he looks for faithful people to make successful. God has gone out of His way to remove the stumbling blocks of our inadequacy. If you feel unworthy of the life God has for you, it's because you are looking at the wrong things. Giftedness, age, status, or your past, have no bearing on your usefulness to God. God looks for an unmixed heart that says, "God, I am available for whatever You want to do in my life."

"...for God sees not as man sees, for man looks at the outward appearance, but the Lord looks at the heart."

(I Samuel 16:7 KJV)

CHAPTER THIRTY-TWO

MAINTAINING A GOOD NAME

Nothing stands still. Life is in constant change, but each of us can change that focus to work for us. Think for a moment of the power of the sun. If all the rays of the sun were concentrated through a magnifying glass on one spot on a fallen log, a fire would ignite within a few minutes and turn that log into fuel for a flame. Yet without a concentrated focus, the sun could shine for decades on the same log and it would remain just an ordinary piece of wood until, over time and under ordinary circumstances, it would simply decompose.

It's the same with you and me. Both success and failure take time, but it takes less time to succeed—as long as you do the right thing rather than the wrong thing. When you work with the right concentrated focus, in the right way, success comes more quickly.

From 1972 through 1995, in the winter months of October through April, we watched our business drop by fifty percent because our product line was limited to latex paint, which is

"It takes less time to succeed than it does to fail."

in less demand. But we saw things change when our Industrial Division began to manufacture solvent-based paints. It was our lifesaver. Now, due to our expanded product line and the growth of our customer base, our business is good year round.

Penn Square Bank went under in 1985, and all hell broke loose as interest rates soared above fifteen percent. And our business did not escape the financial devastation and upheaval either, because we watched as our sales dropped thirty percent. To add to our difficulties, the winter that year was tough, with thirty straight days of temperatures below freezing.

For three weeks, our water pipes froze, and in order for us to continue to make paint, we had to run a garden hose from a nearby building. To keep the hose functional, we had to monitor and move it often. That winter we were forced to lay off a couple of employees and sell some of our pickups to make ends meet.

In '85, we hired a chemist. The year before, we began to produce oil-based paint and were at the point that we needed a production facility, so we built a new one next door. Over the next few years, we were awarded the paint contract for all the state prisons, schools, parks, and other state facilities.

By '92, we had outgrown our location at 1700 W Sheridan, which led us to purchase 1801 West Reno from General Electric. Its forty-two thousand square foot facility houses our latex plant headquarters. It was a good move with one exception. The two factories duplicated many things.

In July of '95, we hired a new chemist, Steve Bussjaeger, who has been with us now for the past seventeen years. His previous experience at Davis Paint in Kansas City, Missouri helped put us in the industrial paint business, and one of our first big accounts was Ditch Witch of Perry, Oklahoma. They sell boring and trenching equipment, which they want painted their signature colors of orange and black. This company has become a valuable client for us since day one and continues to garner our appreciation.

PUT OUT THE FIRE

October 13,1998, was a rare and beautiful fall day with little to no wind. Things were on schedule at work, so about four o'clock that afternoon, I went to the Willow Creek driving range to try out a new set of golf clubs. In the midst of practice, my cell phone rang. It was Cindy, our receptionist. "Joe, the Sheridan plant's on fire!" I looked to the north and could see enormous billows of black smoke ascending straight up into the autumn sky.

Leaving the clubs on the driving range, I ran to my car pleading, "Jesus, Jesus, please put out the fire!" The plant was sixty-four blocks north of my location, and as I drove toward it, the smoke began to turn from black to gray and within a few minutes, it had stopped altogether.

When I arrived, fire trucks crammed the streets and parking lot. The fire started when an

"Jesus, Jesus, please put out the fire!"

employee lowered a large Cowls dissolver, which is a machine used in the manufacturing of paint, into a five-hundred-gallon vat. As the machine descended, an electrical cord was cut which caused a spark that ignited the entire five-hundred-gallon tub of paint. The employee, thankfully, was okay.

The plant, though, was not. The fire had burned a hole through the roof, which proved to be a blessing, because it prevented its spread to the other paint tanks; the adjacent room housed a three thousand gallon tank of naphtha, a solvent that became so hot, the paint blistered off the tank.

It was a miracle of God that the whole plant didn't explode. A fireman told me later, that had he known what was in that plant, he would never have entered the building. We were completely shut down, despite having just accepted a big order from a new customer in Kansas.

The smoke left everything covered in grimy black soot, which required us to hire cleanup crews, who worked around the clock to remove the debris. Our electrician ran temporary lines to some of our mixers so that we could continue to produce paint.

As it turned out, our insurance company had to rebuild the facility to bring it back to code. The cost to rebuild it thirteen years later was considerably more.

When there are fiery trials in life, the enemy's purpose is to destroy us. But God works to mature us and make us stronger. The enemy tries to get us unbalanced and shaken up, because his ultimate goal is to convince us to give up.

Don't let him. Make a decision to put out the fire in your life with God's word, with God's work and in God's way. "And we know that God causes all things to work together for good to those who love God, to those who are called according to His purpose" (Romans 8:28).

KEEP YOUR WORD

Then there was the local company that produced their own furniture for their stores and contracted us to clear-coat their tables and chairs. Our chemist at the time used something called zinc striate in the product to flatten the sheen. But the zinc striate made the clear-coat product water sensitive. The company called to report their tables had water spots, so we drove to Perry, Oklahoma to access the situation, and to assure the company that we would take care of the problem.

They supplied us with a new set of tables and benches to exchange out a store. But therein lay the challenge: the work had to be done after eleven o'clock at night. We took the first load of the refurbished furniture to Perry, removed the old and installed the new.

That night we learned there were fifteen more stores with this same problem. By the time we got home, it was four o'clock in the morning and all six of us had to go to work at the plant four hours later. I said, "Lord, I don't know if I can complete this hellacious project. I need Your help."

The plan was to strip, sand, and apply three coats of lacquer to the furniture and wrap it. Then we had to install it the next

Tuesday night, and four of the stores were located in the Dallas, Ft. Worth area. It was an expensive lesson, but we kept our word and finished the job.

SHUT UP AND KEEP WORKING

Another memorable situation developed with our pool paint at an apartment complex in Stillwater, Oklahoma. The temperature that day was right at 100°F, and as we cleaned and water- blasted the pool, the manager cussed us out the entire time. I wanted to kick his rear end, but God said, "Shut up and keep working."

The pool's problem originated with the pool and not our paint, in that the pool had developed a leak. As we repainted it, we watched water seep in from the bottom. Nevertheless, the manager insisted it was our fault. Boy, it was hard to heed God's words that day, but it paid off in the end. Sometimes, it really is best just to shut up and work.

"A good name is to be more desired than great riches, Favor is better than silver and gold."

(Proverbs 22:1)

CHOOSE RIGHT OVER WRONG

On another occasion, a customer bought a quart of stain and painted a swatch from the sample quart on a new house for the homeowner's review. The homeowner liked the color, so the painter bought four gallons, but the color turned out to be ten times darker, which angered the homeowner.

The fault lay with the painter, who had failed to stir the quart sample before he painted the swatch, but they insisted the error was with our stain. It was not, but we fixed the problem anyway. We put people first before anything else.

ALWAYS BE HONEST

Then there was the year we had a problem with some of our paint shipped to Canada intended for use on farm equipment. The temperature registered below -30°F, sleeting rain, and our paint cold checked (cracked) on their equipment. The cost to sandblast and repaint the farm equipment was $160,000. I assured the company we would take care of the problem and we did. The next week they quit us. I told the customer, "I have never beaten anyone out of any money and I won't start with you."

BE A GRACIOUS PROBLEM-SOLVER

Another situation developed, similar to the one above, with a company in Kansas. Again, we stood by our product, took care of the problem, and the company continues to be a valuable client to this day.

Over the years we've had our share of problems. Some of them were our fault and some were the fault of the painter. But we've always given the customer the benefit of the doubt.

PUT GOD FIRST

When I bought the I-40 and Penn property, I hired a sign painter, right off the bat, to emblazon "CHRIST IS THE ANSWER – JOHN 14:6" on the north side of the building which faced the heavily trafficked interstate I-40 highway. Since that time, we have received many cards and letters from strangers, who have commented that the sign made a difference in their day.

"Christ is the answer."

Once, a young lady called from the bus station in downtown Oklahoma City. She was from Florida and said, "My boyfriend and I got into a fight at the airport, and I'm on my way to the bus station. While en route to the bus station, the cab driver drove by your place twice, and your sign caught my attention. Maybe Christ is who I need."

So I had my receptionist drive to the bus station and lead her to the Lord. To this day, I have never had a negative comment about the sign.

My hope is that everyone who sees the sign will think, These people are genuine and take care of their customers.

Our location at 1801 W. Reno.

The Lord has blessed us with good and loyal employees. I learned early on that if you pay your employees well and treat them with respect, they, in turn, respond in kind. Your company will be successful.

For His eyes are upon the ways of a man, and He sees all his steps... The steps of a man are established by the LORD; and He delights in his way.

(Job 34:21; Psalm 37:23)

CHAPTER THIRTY-THREE

A PANTONE OF EXPERIENCE

GOD KNOWS THE DESIRES OF YOUR HEART

In '74, the early days of the company, I painted houses to have extra money for our vacations. In one of those times, a friend's house in Midwest City needed to be painted. In the process of my work on his house, I commented, "This is a nice neighborhood. I like it."

He said, "The house across the street will be up for sale soon, because the couple's filed for a divorce."

When Dorothy came by with my lunch that day, I told her about the house and asked her to knock on the door and give them my business card. A week later, the woman called and asked, "Would you like to see it?"

We drove over, walked through it, and I asked her, "How much do you want for it?"

She said, "We have $700 equity in it. The house is three thousand square feet and the price is $37,000." It was in poor condition, but a great buy. We moved in the next month, and it proved to be an ideal place for us to raise our three boys. We built a pool in the backyard, had friends over and many church youth parties there.

DON'T TRY TO BE SMARTER THAN GOD

In 1984, we bought the builders' new, fully furnished showcase house in the Greenbriar-Kingswood addition located at Penn and SW 104.

However, there was one problem: we still had to sell our house in Midwest City. The home we had bought for $37,000 now appraised for $155,000. A neighbor two doors down offered me $135,000 the first week it was on the market, but our realtor advised me to hold out for $155,000. It turned out to be a big mistake. I had that house for the next five years and in the end, sold it for $95,000.

> "We must be good stewards of our blessings and careful not to let our blessings crowd God out of our life."

In '92, we moved again into another new house in the same area, but this one was on a greenbelt, which made it ideal for our dogs: Honey, a cocker spaniel; Sugar, a black and tan stray; and Lucy, a yellow lab. All our children and grandchildren lived nearby.

We must be good stewards of our blessings and careful not to let our blessings crowd God out of our life. Make every effort to keep God first at all times.

Bailey Smith, Joe Cox, Marvin Starkey and the $15,000 shovel.

During that time, First Southern Baptist Church Del City was buying the property at Sooner Road and SW 29 Street. Brother Bailey Smith needed cash, so I borrowed $15,000 from the bank and donated it to the building fund. I was certain God would sell our house, which would enable us to pay off the note. I learned the hard way that God really didn't care about my bargain. I wound up putting the $15,000 on a monthly payment plan for three years.

The lesson I learned: Don't presume upon God.

BE A LIFELONG LEARNER

Soon after we were saved, Dorothy and I attended Bill Gothard's Basic Youth Conflicts Institute. It was a forty-hour, weeklong teaching session held once a year that covered important life challenges. Like dry sponges, we absorbed those life-changing lessons on ways to handle conflict from a Christian worldview. Over the years, we must have attended the conference at least ten times.

Many of my daily decisions go back to things I learned in those sessions; among which was the importance of following the chain of authority. Gothard explained that authority is like an "umbrella of protection," and when we get out from under it, we expose ourselves to unnecessary temptations, which are often too strong for us to overcome.

This is why Scripture compares rebellion with witchcraft: "Rebellion is like the sin of witchcraft" (I Samuel 15:23 KJV). Both terms have the same basic definition—subjecting ones self to the realm and power of Satan.

USE WHAT YOU KNOW

Our friends Larry and Gina Norris facilitated various Bible studies in their home, among which was "Marriage Without Regret." One evening, our study's focus was Ephesians 5:22-25. It read, "Husbands, love your wives, just as Christ also loved the church and gave Himself up for her."

On the way home, I pondered the discussion generated by the passage, because at this stage in our marriage, I didn't even like Dorothy, much less love her enough to die for her. I asked the Lord that night to give me a desire to love and care for my wife like the Bible instructed. If God could deliver me from alcohol and cigarettes, He could surely restore my love for Dorothy.

Up to this point, our marriage mirrored the role reversal my parents had used in their marriage. Mom ran the show and Dad was the playboy. When I married, I expected my wife to slip into that same role. My role as a husband was undefined and I resented Dorothy, because she took over. But she did so out of necessity; she was forced to fill my God-designed role, because I didn't.

PAINT OUTSIDE THE LINES

I know now that my wife and marriage are a gift from God, but the first twelve years were tough. Marriage didn't come with a handbook of instructions, and I was clueless about the different rolls that came with the package. I didn't know how to be a husband, let alone a father. In spite of it all, however, to Dorothy's credit, she stayed with me through those growing-up years.

We had a rocky-road beginning: I was eighteen and in high school, Dorothy was nineteen and pregnant. No one gave our marriage a sliver of a hope that it would stand the test of time. As you've learned throughout this book, in our first few years, we had more than our share of problems.

Although, God changed both our lives back in April of '72, we still had much to learn and implement. I realized I had a diamond in the rough and didn't know it. Proverbs 18:22, my version, "A good wife is more desirable than great riches." She prayed for me daily and encouraged me to keep my chin up and my faith strong. We also prayed together.

In the formative years of the company, I brought problems home in the evenings and unloaded them on Dorothy. She tried to help me solve them, but soon realized what I needed most was for someone to just listen. And she became good at that.

TAKE TIME TO BE THANKFUL

Walking on the beach, wherever the beach might be, is one of Dorothy's favorite get-a-ways. Over the years, we grew closer and seemed to be able to read each other's minds, which I guess is what happens when you've been with someone you love for fifty-five years. She is my best friend. Each day, we make it a priority is to build each other up and look for opportunities to honor and respect each other. Some days we fail, but we're quick to recover. God, in His grace, has chosen to bless us and we are humbled and most grateful.

Charm is deceitful and beauty is vain, but a woman who fears the LORD, she shall be praised.
(Proverbs 31:30)

Early in our marriage, I lived with major blind spots, and it was God's word that gave me insight and revealed errors in my thinking, along with principles which enabled me to be the kind of husband He wanted me to be. It saddens me when I hear people say, "The Bible is outdated." That could not be further from the truth. The words of Scripture are alive and saturated with the power of God. His word is a source of strength, which provides wisdom and guidance for every struggle we will ever face.

For the commandment is a lamp, and the teaching, is light; And reproofs for discipline are the way of life.
(Proverbs 6:23)

CHAPTER THIRTY-FOUR

THE COLOR OF GREEN

I love golf, which means, like most golfers, my dream was to attend the Masters in Augusta, Georgia. In fact, I love the Masters so much that I had a green sports coat, custom-made and identical to the one the Masters champions receive. I wear it on special occasions and it looks great with my bright yellow shirt.

One day, Tom Elliff called to say, "I have an opportunity to play the Augusta National Golf Course." He had a friend who lived in Augusta, who, while not a member, had clients who were. I said, "Tom, if you are ever allowed to bring a friend, I'll go anytime."

Tom and myself at Augusta.

A year later, Dorothy and I, along with our friends John and Kathy Patton, were in Palm Springs, California on a golf outing. On Wednesday, my phone rang. It was Tom who called to say, "We have a one o'clock, tee time Monday in Augusta."

That Monday morning, we flew to Augusta and met Tom's friend, who invited us to have lunch at the Augusta National Clubhouse, an exclusive, members-only club. It is next to impossible to even gain access to the club's grounds, and yet there we were, eating a meal and playing one of the most hallowed courses in golf history. Tom, his friend, the member, and I had a wonderful time. I shot an 89, with 39 putts and one birdie. Before leaving, I splurged in their gift shop and bought all kinds of shirts, balls, and souvenirs. But still, nothing they had there was as great as my green jacket.

Three years later, Tom's friend invited us to the actual Masters Tournament. He had tickets for Monday through Sunday for Dorothy and I, John and Kathy Patton, and Tom and Jeannie Elliff. It was 1999, and the year Jose Maria Olazabal won the tournament. It was a dream come true.

MY SUNDAY CONVICTION

An unshakable belief is a conviction you hold so deeply that you have no need for proof or evidence.

About thirty years ago, I led a man to Christ and the following Sunday morning, when he arrived at church, he requested to be baptized. The baptismal service was scheduled for eleven o'clock that morning, which presented a problem for me. I had previously registered to play in Wewoka's Annual Member-Guest Golf Tournament, which was sixty-five miles away, with a shotgun start at one o'clock.

I could not leave, because I was responsible for him even being there. And I wanted to share this monumental moment in his walk with the Lord. But as soon as he was baptized, I made a mad dash to my car and drove to Wewoka at a breakneck speed of eighty miles an hour.

My first hole was number 7, a par 3. I topped the ball and it sailed about 30 yards landing in a ditch. I had to lay it out for a one-stroke penalty. Later, I was hitting 3 on a par 3 hole when my next shot went over the green. My fourth shot fell short of the green, but with my fifth shot, I finally managed to get on to the green and two-putted for 7. I had a terrible game and finished last in my flight.

On the drive back to Oklahoma City, I mulled over my lackluster performance on the golf course that afternoon and excused it with the thought that it was due to my hurried circumstances. It never occurred to me that God might not want me to play golf on Sunday.

At the time, I also taught a men's class at our church, and at half past five on Sunday afternoon, Dorothy and I attended a teachers' meeting. The Bible says that we should have a day of rest, but church plus golf made my Sunday's long and tiring.

> "It never occurred to me that God might not want me to play golf on Sunday"

The next month, I was in a tournament at Willow Creek with a shotgun start set for noon, so I hurried through Sunday School and skipped church altogether. On the first hole, my shot went left and out of bounds. First penalty, I was now hitting the number 3. Again, it went out of bounds to the left and added another penalty for not hitting number 5. It went right out of bounds. Now hitting number 7 on the first tee box on a par 5 hole, I made a disastrous 12 on the hole.

With back-to-back Sunday golf tournament disasters, it finally crossed my mind that God might not want me to play golf on Sunday. So I asked Him, "Do You not want me to play on Sunday?" I'm sure He must have laughed and thought, You finally figured it out, big boy.

On that day, I made the decision never to play golf on Sunday again, and because of that conviction, I miss a lot of our club's tournaments. But I believe God wants me to give my Sundays to Him.

I don't mean to say that it's wrong to play golf on Sunday; I believe it's just wrong for me, and it is an unshakable belief.

Learn to be happy with your life. God intentionally designed everything about you, so delight yourself in the way that He made you. Don't complain, don't compare, and don't covet. Instead, delight yourself in your talents, your skills, and your hobbies. Decide to enjoy your life, because He is not going to give you someone else's.

Delight yourself in the Lord; and He will give you the desires of your heart. (Psalm 37:4)

CHAPTER THIRTY-FIVE

NEVER GIVE UP ON GOD

In '76, my family, my sister's family, our friends, Dan and Dorothy Wallace, and their sons, Jeff and Danny, drove to California for a vacation. We spent one night in Las Vegas, and to this day that remains my one and only night in that city. As a four-year-old Christian, I knew that place would be trouble for me. And it would still prove to be trouble for me forty years later.

On the way back from California, I asked to ride along with Dan. His marriage was in trouble and I wanted to encourage him. He told me he didn't need my God because he had his own. He went on to say, "Your God's for weak men and old ladies." So I shut up. He later divorced his wife and during the next thirty years, I saw him maybe ten times.

GOD NEVER GIVES UP ON US

One Saturday, a friend called to tell me that Dan had cancer and was scheduled for surgery at Oklahoma City's Mercy Hospital the next week. I visited him in the pre-op room and said, "Dan, could I pray for you?"

He said, "Yes." After I prayed, they wheeled him into surgery. Over the next few months, he underwent treatment and we talked by phone, but schedule conflicts never seemed to allow us to get together for anything more substantive.

Dorothy and I were in Palm Springs on another golf outing, when I received a call and learned that Dan's condition was now

Dorothy and myself with our friends John and Kathy Patton.

critical. I called his house and spoke with his wife, who told me that he was too sick to talk and that she was putting him in the hospital over the Memorial Day weekend. We returned from Palm Springs around 8 o'clock Friday evening, and our route home from the airport took us by Baptist Hospital.

I said, "Dorothy, I need to stop and see Dan," so we pulled into the visitors' parking area, parked and went up to the cancer ward on the seventh floor. I located his room, went in, and found him alone, sitting up in bed.

I said, "Dan."

He looked up and said, "Joe?"

"Do you know why I'm here?"

"Yes," he said. "You want me to go to heaven with you."

I asked, "Do you want to go to heaven?"

He said, "Yes."

My heart leapt as I prayed with him and led him through the sinner's prayer: Romans 3:23 states that "we all have sinned and

> **"Do you want to go to heaven?"**

fall short of the glory of God," but "God so loved the world, that

He gave His only begotten Son, that whoever believes in Him shall not perish, but have eternal life" (John 3:16).

And Romans 10:9-10 says, that "if you confess with your mouth Jesus as Lord, and believe in your heart that God raised Him from the dead, you will be saved; for with the heart a person believes, resulting in righteousness, and with the mouth he confesses, resulting in salvation." The three steps are:

1. Admit that you are a sinner.
2. Believe in your heart that Jesus died for your sins and God raised Him from the dead.
3. Confess with your mouth Jesus is Lord.

Afterwards, I went out to the waiting room to get Dorothy and we returned to Dan's room where I shared the good news that Dan had received Christ as his Savior. I was grateful that I had heeded the Holy Spirit's prompt to drop by, and Dorothy was happy for both of us.

Dorothy told him that she had prayed for his salvation for thirty years. She asked, "Dan, would you like for Joe to stay with you through the night?" He said he would, so Dorothy went home and left us; we stayed up half the night reconnecting and talking about old times.

Never give up on people, because God never gives up on anyone.

Dan died two days later. I can't wait to see him again.

For I am confident of this one thing, that He who began a good work in you will perfect it until the day of Jesus Christ. (Philippians 1:6)

CHAPTER THIRTY-SIX

THE BUSINESS OF LIFE

At one point shortly, after we'd gotten H-I-S Paint off the ground, Dorothy's mom, Christine, and her husband, Gene, were in financial trouble They lived in Columbus, Ohio, so I sent them some money, but not before I said to Dorothy, "If I am going to support them, they need to move to Oklahoma City."

They agreed and one Friday, one of my drivers and I drove a truck to Columbus and loaded up their things. We brought them to Oklahoma City where I had rented an apartment for them. In an effort to help Gene establish a financial footing, I hired him as a salesman, but unfortunately he did not want to follow the company's protocol.

Alcohol had such a grip on Gene's life that it was next to impossible for him to hold a steady job. Besides that, he was verbally and physically abusive to Christine, but the final breaking point came one day, when word got back to me that one of our trucks had seen parked outside a bar. He tried to convince me that he was talking with a customer, but I knew better.

The next morning I called their apartment and said, "Gene, I need you to come by the office today."

He replied, "I can't, I have an appointment in Guthrie."

"Gene, come by the office in the morning."

He insisted that he couldn't. So, with heavy hearts, Dorothy and I drove to their apartment complex where I fired him and collected the keys to the company truck.

Before long, he and Christine parted ways and divorced.

At the time, our pastor at First Southern Baptist Church Del City was Bailey Smith. Sometime after this incident, he went with me to visit Christine, shared the gospel with her, and led her to the Lord, much to our family's delight.

Then there was the time in '79 when I bought a new Ford custom van with an extended cab, painted silver and blue like the colors used by the Dallas Cowboys, my favorite football team. It commanded the road, driving like a slightly smaller shipping crate, but completely done up inside to deliver every comfort and luxury you could want on a long trip. It included some oh-so-fashionable shag carpeting.

Whenever we traveled into the mountains on snow skiing trips, we drove that van. One day, we were in Wewoka, riding around with my family, and an argument broke out between Dad and my brother, Jim. Harsh words were exchanged, and it got so bad that Dad demanded I take him home, where he stormed into the house mad as a wet hen.

I followed Dad into the house and tried to share the Lord with him. I said, "Someday you will die, and when I walk by your casket, I want to know that you're in heaven."

He said, "Don't worry about it, son. I'm not ready to change yet."

I responded, "Dad, every time I see you, from now till you die, I'm going to ask you to accept Christ."

> **"Someday you are going to die, and when I walk by your casket, I want to know that you're in heaven."**

Three days later, he and Mom came to Oklahoma City. Dad said he wanted to buy a diamond ring like mine, so I took him to the jewelry store and he bought a ring. Afterwards, I invited them to come to our house for supper that evening. When they arrived, the first words out of his mouth were, "Son, I want what you have with God." Those words were music to my ears.

He prayed to receive Christ that evening in our kitchen. And years later when he died, I walked by his casket with the confident assurance that he was in heaven, and someday I would see him again.

Our trip to Hawaii with Mom and Dad and Dorothy's Mom.

Mother suffered with leukemia during the last few years of her life. And to celebrate her eightieth birthday, Dorothy and I took her, Dad, and Dorothy's mom, Christine, to Hawaii. Mother died two years later. That is one memorable trip I have never regretted.

Precious in the sight of the Lord, is the death of His godly ones. (Psalm 116:15)

CHAPTER THIRTY-SEVEN

PAINTING THE WORLD

Joe McCuen, a friend of ours, sold chemicals in Beijing, China, and convinced me he could sell them our paint. February 15, 2002, Dorothy and I, my brother Johnny, and Joe McCuen flew to Beijing, where we met with his contact, Ms. Ma, a hardworking, well-educated Chinese woman in her mid-forties.

L to R: Johnny, Dorothy, Myself, Chen Tau, Big Joe McCuen and Ms. Ma

Ms. Ma had arranged for an interpreter, Chen Tau, who attended the University of Beijing, to accompany us during our time in China. Dorothy talked with Ms. Ma through Chen Tau about the Lord and before it was over, Dorothy gifted Ms. Ma with her Bible, which included her notes, handwritten in the margins, taken over many years of Bible study. Dorothy's treasure became Ms. Ma's treasure.

WORK TO BRING LIFE TO OTHERS

Ms. Ma took us to meet with the Mayor of Beijing, which eventually resulted in a contract to ship containers of our paint to China. Back in Oklahoma: we filled containers with our paint, shipped them by truck to Ft. Worth, Texas, where they were loaded onto a train bound for Long Beach, California, and then transported by freighter to Tianjin, China, a port about one hundred miles north of Beijing.

In all, the transport took about thirty days. After negotiations were completed, Kent and I signed a joint venture agreement with the Chinese on April 8, 2005.

Prior to the trip, Ms. Ma had sent us our itinerary, which included the time and location for Sunday morning church service. On Sunday, we were taken to a large room in a hotel where about thirty people had gathered. The songs and preaching were in Chinese, and when their pastor finished, I was invited to say a few words. With the help of an interpreter, I made the most of the opportunity and shared my testimony.

Afterwards, I asked the group, "What do you do for a living?" We learned they were all professionals—doctors, lawyers, and business people. I asked them how long they had been believers, and each one's story was the same: they had followed the Lord less than three years.

First trip coming home from Beijing. Dorothy went shopping.

A few years later, Ms. Ma and Chen Tau came to the United States and visited us in Oklahoma. She told us about her friend in Hong Kong, who taught a course in religion at the University of Hong Kong. Chen Tau had given her friend Dorothy's Bible to teach from. It was very meaningful, but as of this writing, Chen Tau has not accepted Christ. Undaunted, we continue to pray that the Lord will open the eyes and ears of her understanding and give her a hunger to know Jesus, the one true God.

The following year, Ms. Ma made her second trip to Oklahoma. Upon her arrival, she communicated immediately, through her interpreter, her desire to attend church with us on Sunday and be baptized. Another Chinese woman in our church learned of Ms. Ma's recent salvation experience and offered to help with her baptismal request.

Ms. Ma was baptized at First Southern Baptist Church Del City, and is an encouraging example to us of God's ability to work even in a difficult situation such as a Communist country. He is not bound by ordinances and a false belief system.

"Is anything too difficult for the Lord?" Genesis 18:14

LIVE BEYOND YOUR DREAMS

Since then, we have traveled to China many times. But due to the lengthy transport time and import duties assessed to our paint, we began manufacturing it there in '09. And Kent and I were privileged to made the first batch of paint in Beijing, China, reminiscent of the first batch I made thirty-seven years earlier on SE 26 Street. Back then I never dreamed I would ever even visit China much less make a batch of paint there. But the Lord's plans for those who follow Him go far beyond anything we could ever think, hope, or imagine.

In '08, I met Lyn Anglin, a man from Georgia, who sold building materials in Abu Dhabi and Dubai in the United Arab Emirates. He had a trip planned there two weeks later and wanted to take some of our literature with him. So I gave him a packet, which detailed all of our product information and sent him off, with low expectations.

Lyn called me from Abu Dhabi on a Tuesday and said, "Joe, they want to fly you over here to discuss building a paint factory." The following Sunday, September 14, Dorothy and I boarded a British Airways flight headed for Abu Dhabi. Lyn met us at the airport and took us to the Emirates Palace, a seven-star hotel located on the Persian Gulf with beautiful white sandy beaches and warm blue water.

We have never experienced anything like that in our lives and probably never will again. It was the most expensive hotel ever built at a cost of three billion dollars, and is used by the members of the United Arab Emirates for their annual meeting.

It is also the hotel of choice for world leaders and dignitaries from other countries.

Sheikh Khalifa Bin Zayed's business manager arranged for our stay at the Palace Hotel, and he and his wife joined us for dinner that evening (incidentally, we found it interesting to note that she was fashionably dressed western style, though whether

The Emirates Palace Hotel in Abu Dhabi.

that was a regular occurrence for her or just something she did for our benefit remains a mystery). The next day, they took us to the Sheikh's polo fields, but due to Ramadan, there was an imposed fast from seven o'clock in the morning until seven o'clock in the evening.

During our stay, Dorothy was stopped in the hotel lobby by one of the hotel guards, who told her that due to Ramadan, she was not allowed to carry her bottle of water with her in public. They also did not approve of a woman walking in the hotel unaccompanied by her husband.

The next day, we discussed business and at the end of the conversation, I agreed to send them our proposal for the plant. After the meeting, we took a limousine to Dubai, located one hundred miles south via a modern freeway lined with palm trees and streetlights.

The city was pristinely beautiful and all their buildings were newly constructed. In the United Arab Emirates, all automobiles older than seven years are sent to Africa. Once in Dubai, we checked into the exquisite Grand Kempinski Hotel, which houses many amazing things, including an indoor snow-ski run. The amount of energy required to support this lavish playground almost boggles the mind: 100°F outside, and snow-ski runs inside.

That evening, we had dinner in the Burj Khalifa hotel, the one shaped like a sailboat and also the one Tom Cruise dangled from in the film Mission: Impossible – Ghost Protocol. It is, at the time of this writing, also the world's tallest man-made structure. The hotel's strict policy prohibits any one from entering the hotel with out dinner reservation. Dorothy and I each ordered a steak, salad and desert for a total cost of $500 U.S. dollars.

As an avid golfer, I watch a lot of the sport on television, and every time I saw Tiger Woods play in a tournament on the Dubai golf course, I would say to Dorothy, "Someday I am going to play that course." And I did. The Emirates Country Club Golf Course is the same course Woods plays every year in the televised tournament so, for me, this was the trip of a lifetime.

God knows how to get you from where you are and take you to places you never thought you would be. As long as you have hope, you hold on to a future that is filled with good things.

For I know the plans that I have for you, declares the LORD, plans for welfare and not for calamity, to give you a future and a hope. (Jeremiah 29:11)

CHAPTER THIRTY-EIGHT

ENJOY YOUR FAMILY

Our first family vacation was a three-day trip to Turner Falls, Oklahoma's largest waterfall, located in southern Oklahoma's famous Arbuckle Mountains in 1965. This is Oklahoma's oldest state park, and its waterfall gushes down a seventy-seven foot drop. Its been compared to the Grand Canyon and the Black Hills, because the terrain offers a historic view into the geologic past.

Dorothy and I, together with Kent, Kirk, Tony, stayed in a $20-a-night motel in Sulphur, located just off I-35 between Oklahoma City and Dallas. We took an ice chest packed with lunchmeat, cereal, bread, and milk, but treated ourselves to a restaurant meal once a day. The waterfall was beautiful and we swam in the natural pool formed at the base of the falls—all in all, a wonderful time together as a family.

Kent, Kirk and Tony at South Padre Island in 1967.

The next year we drove down to Corpus Christi, Texas and followed the same meal plan as the year before. It was the first of about fifteen trips to the Gulf of Mexico and the

Doing a little fishing.

Padre Island with the boys.

site of many wonderful vacations, sunburns, sand castles, and fishing.

During one vacation to South Padre Island, I sold a thousand gallons of paint to a new condominium complex, which was under construction at the time. That called for a couple of return trips that year.

By this point, our family had grown, and our boys had gotten married and had children of their own. Kent and Kelly

Destin, Florida trip.

recommended we make Destin, Florida the site of our next beach trip. They had visited it, and their description of the beautiful white sandy beaches sold Dorothy and me. And for the next fifteen years, this became our vacation destination. Every July, all twenty-one of us headed for Destin, where many great memories were made. The kids loved to go with their cousins and play on the beach.

Kent is married to Kelly and they have two children, Kristen and Jeremy. Kristen is now grown and married to Jon Echols, and they have three children; David, Ethan,

Playing in the sand, Destin, Florida.

and Kaylee. Jeremy is married to Jessica, and they have four children; Adyson, Landon, Hudson, and Capton.

Kirk is married to Diane, and they have three children; Courtney, Caleb, and Alexis. Courtney is married to Jon Graves.

Tony, our youngest son, is married to Beth, and they have eight children; Carter, Joel, Britton, Talbot, Emily, Garrett, Macy, and Claire.

Behold, children are a gift of the LORD; the fruit of the womb is a reward. Like arrows in the hand of a warrior, so are the children of ones youth. How blessed is the man whose quiver is full of them; they shall not be ashamed, when they speak with their enemies in the gate.

(Psalm 127:3-5)

Other vacation spots have included: Cabo San Lucas, Aruba, St. Thomas, and Hawaii. Our family and grandkids love the beach, and it could be said that we're a bunch of beach bums. Life is too short not to enjoy fun trips together as a family. Tony's wife Beth plans all our vacations, which is no small feat for a group as large as ours. But as an authorized Disney Vacation Planner and owner of Hourglass Travel and Events, she's honed her skills and handles every trip like a walk in the park.

I encourage my employees to make their families a priority, and show them they are a priority: take them on vacations, and spend quality time with them. And I make every effort to provide a work environment, which will enable them to do just that.

ELVIS HAS LEFT THE BUILDING

In the early nineties, I had some frequent flyer airline miles that were about to expire. After scanning a map of the United States, I concluded that Seattle was the farthest point they could take us. Earlier, Dorothy had read an article in the National Geographic Magazine written by a man who had taken a train from Vancouver to Banff, Lake Louise, the Ice fields, Jasper, and through the game reserve. It looked and sounded like a grand adventure, so we decided to give it a try.

We flew to Seattle, rented a car, and drove to Vancouver. However, I underestimated the ease in procuring hotel reservations. Upon our arrival, we stopped at the first nice-looking motel, and discovered they were booked, as was the next motel in which we inquired.

Desperate, I said to the woman at the desk, "My wife is fuming mad at my failure." She took pity on me, made some calls, and located The Blue Boy, which was about four miles down the road. As we approached, we saw a big neon sign shaped like a singer that resembled Elvis Presley. Located in a seedy part of town, I parked the car and told Dorothy to lock the doors.

The woman at the desk, which joined a bar peopled with a noisy crowd, rented me a room. I asked her, "Where do I park my car?" She directed me to a large garage behind the motel. I went to the car, got Dorothy and the luggage, and told her to stand by the front desk until I returned.

I found the garage, quickly parked the car, and returned to the front desk where I had stationed Dorothy, who had been, in my brief absence, propositioned by a drunk at the bar. We found our room upstairs whose windows led out to the building's roof. We rolled the dresser up to the window, and shoved a couch against the door.

The Chateau at Lake Louise.

The next day, we started the route Dorothy had read about in the National Geographic Magazine, drove to Lake Louise and checked into a room at the Chateau at Lake Louise. Our new accommodations garnered our utmost appreciation and the unbridled refrain, "This is a far cry from the Blue Boy Motel," flowed from our lips as we took in the grandiose facility.

The next morning, we hiked a scenic trail and lunched under the majestic towering peaks of the Canadian Rockies. Lake Louise was breathtakingly beautiful, so we rented a canoe and paddled across its emerald waters, then lunched the next day at Banff. The following day, we drove the Icefield Parkway, past the Athabasca Glacier and Ice Fields, and on to Jasper. On our return trip, we stayed one night at the Fairmont Empress Hotel in Victoria British Columbia and enjoyed high tea in the afternoon.

The next morning, we loaded the car and boarded a ferry back to Seattle. When we arrived at the dock, I feasted on clams. While our spontaneous trip failed to include a plan, we still managed to wing it and have the time of our lives.

Make a decision to laugh along the way, stay sweet in your spirit, and persevere.

But you, be strong and do not lose courage, for there is reward for your work. (II Chronicles 15:7)

CHAPTER THIRTY-NINE

TRIPS WITH A MISSION

From its inception, our company has maintained a heart for other countries of the world. Whether we donate our time or give financially, we support mission outreaches. At one time, we had an opportunity to donate six hundred gallons of paint for schools and churches in Ghana, Africa.

In 2011, I traveled once more to Beijing, but this time I went with a group of Christian businessmen from Oklahoma to visit factory churches and speak to the Chinese Christian businessmen. I offered to help them if ever there was a need. I also met Ms. Ma's good friend, who was in a great church. My what a tremendous blessing it was to experience God at work in areas of the world, which forbids His free gift of Love.

Another opportunity came my way when a group from the Southern Baptist Convention's Disaster Relief program traveled to Guatemala. We flew to Guatemala City, and were transported to Tecpan, a modern Mayan town located about one hundred miles south of Guatemala City. A large earthquake had destroyed the community and we were the third crew to arrive from the United States to help rebuild a church. My job was to put ninety-pound bags of cement and sand into a portable cement mixer.

Conditions were rough, but we knew that when we signed up for the project. But head knowledge is a far cry from reality. Our housing accommodations were primitive. We had no electricity or running water and slept in small pup tents. The ladies of the church prepared our meals on a grill made from the lid of a fifty-five-gallon barrel drum. We were there five days before we were able to bathe, and when a man from the community offered to let us use his shower and water well, we accepted his offer without hesitation.

When we left the United States, I had taken three boxes of granola bars and lived on those bars the entire week we were there. The main staple of the Guatemalan diet was black beans and rice, and to this day, I refuse to eat black beans or granola bars.

Helping build a new church in Guatemala.

One night, during our stay, we were treated to a special dinner of tamales, although I had no idea what they used for meat. Plus, with no clean water to drink, we quenched our thirst with bottles of room temperature Pepsi at five cents each.

At a church service one night, a singing group signed and sang Psalm 150, during which, a quiet hush fell over the congregants as the Presence of the Holy Spirit blanketed the service. Psalms 150 is the final psalm in the book of Psalms, and I think it's there by design . . . because the end result of our life is to worship God. No matter what life contains, our final response is to worship God with our whole life.

It was an amazing experience to see this community, who outwardly had so very little of this world's goods, worship the Lord with such genuine, sincere, and joyful exuberance. Their love for God shined through their faces and touched all of us. There was not a dry eye among us.

Praise the Lord! Praise God in His sanctuary; Praise Him for His mighty expanse. Praise Him for His mighty deeds; Praise Him according to His excellent greatness. Praise Him with trumpet sound; Praise Him with harp and lyre. Praise Him with timbrel and dancing; Praise Him with stringed instruments and pipe. Praise Him with loud cymbals; Praise Him with resounding cymbals. Let everything that has breath praise the Lord. Praise the Lord. Praise the Lord! (Psalm 150)

I make it a point each day to remember that God is the source of everything in my life, and as long as I draw breath, I will praise Him and thank Him.

The closer I get to God the more gracious I become. My motive to help others does not come from a place of pity, but comes from the depths of my love and faith in God.

He who despises his neighbor sins, but happy is he who is gracious to the poor. (Proverbs 14:21)

CHAPTER FORTY

CHRIST IS STILL THE ANSWER

There are those who have knowledge and talent, but yet fail to succeed. They know what to do and how to do it but they just don't feel like doing it. They lack inspiration and follow through.

Inspiration that leads to action is the most important ingredient for success in any human endeavor, and it can be developed at will. The person who is inspired to work at whatever is placed before him can overcome any obstacle.

A glance back over my life confirms the truth of God's loving promises to bless those who love Him, honor Him, and serve Him. It has proven to be true for me and for my family; for without Him, we are nothing, but with Him we are everything. Knowing and following Christ is a way of life for us.

Early on, my three competitive sons took an interest in learning the family business, but having them work together has not been with out its challenges. Each of them brings a unique perspective to the company and over the years, we've learned how to utilize their specific visions. A business seminar we once attended recommended we separate the three boys into three different divisions of the company.

In 1988, Business Consultant Ron Kozak was hired to be in charge of our monthly meetings and to keep everyone accountable. A valuable asset to the company, he has promoted a cohesive atmosphere and helped eliminate strife. If we have a difference of opinion, Ron leads the discussion and enables everyone to work through the process. This system, once implemented, has worked well for us.

We separated the company's responsibilities into three parts: Kent has been with H-I-S since 1975 and is Chief Financial Officer and VP of Operations. Kirk joined the company in 1986 and is VP over the Architectural Coating Division. Tony joined the company in 1987 and is VP of the Industrial Coating Division.

Even though I've been successful in business and in life, this kind of success was never my goal. Since my life's beginnings were hard and the middle of my life rough in a different way, one of my aims in life has been to eliminate destructive influences which hold potential problems: the choice in people I associate with, the places I go, alcohol, and cigarettes. I was living in the worst mess a person could live in. My goal was to create an environment where I could serve God.

I had one priority, and Jesus stated it best in Matthew 6:33: "Seek first the kingdom and all these things will be added to you." It's about having that one priority—Jesus, Who, makes everything else possible.

Many people are unhappy and dissatisfied with life because their priorities are out of order. There are many things that we can give our time and attention to, many of

> **"It's about having that one priority - Jesus, Who, makes everything else possible."**

which are not bad. But even good things can get us off track, and sometimes priorities can become a problem.

Living life in reverse is the problem. We go after: a job, money, house, car, and a family. Then hope we will be happy with what we manage to get and in the process, we lose our way and lose sight of why are doing what we are doing. To "seek first" means to flip it around: To make Jesus the first priority.

After all, a couple can't have a good marriage if Jesus isn't front and center. In fact, all of our relationships suffer, if Jesus isn't the source of our love. Money is a mess without Jesus at the front of our finances, and our thoughts and emotions get cluttered without Him.

To seek first means to find out how God wants things done. Find out what He wants from your marriage. Find out what God wants from your career. Find out how God wants you to treat people. Find out what kinds of attitudes we are to have in all things that concern our life.

The first priority is not money, education, status, skill, or even, and I hate to say it, cars, because junkyards the world over are filled with objects of desire that didn't stand the test of time. Think for a moment about your priorities. Your priorities reveal what is first in your life. Put Christ first, above everything else, if you want to have peace and find life's meaning. If God is first, you will have success. I'm living proof that it works.

Before I got my priorities straight, I was a wreck. My attitude was terrible. My habits were out of control. My marriage was a mess. I was full of bitterness and resentment, and all the negativity strangled the peace out of me. When I became a believer, I understood the simple fact that Jesus loved me.

From that point on, all I wanted to do was to live faithfully for Him. Once my priorities were in the right order, "all these things were added" to me. I have a beautiful wife, a wonderful family and a successful business. Those were never my goals. Giving Jesus first place puts everything else in perspective. I made living for Him my priority and He took care of the rest.

The way I see it, everyone has two choices. You can worry and struggle through life or you can put Jesus first and allow Him to take care of your needs. He's made a promise to add good things to your life, if you'll seek him first. After all these years, I can say with all my heart CHRIST IS STILL THE ANSWER.

A cord of three strands is not quickly torn apart.
(Ecclesiastes 4:12)

Me and my three sons with our products.

Our Executive Team.

CHAPTER FORTY-ONE

THE GOLD STANDARD

Kent

I started work at H-I-S from almost the very beginning in —1972; I was fourteen years old. Many days, Dad picked me up from school and took me to work with him. I am probably one of the few people at H-I-S that has done about every job there is to do, whether it's to deliver products, make batches of paint, manage a store, or fulfill accounting duties.

Having previous experience in each of these areas has enabled me to perform my job in operations today and has helped me to see the overall big picture. It is vital that each area of the company fulfill its role and a necessity that each area do its job correctly, because each area impacts the process of the whole company.

After I graduated from high school in 1976, I married my wife, Kelly, and began full time work at H-I-S, mainly in the warehouse which included paint deliveries. In 1978, Dad moved me into management at a store we acquired in Midwest City, an old Glidden Paint store that had been in business for several years.

The store sold wallpaper, Glidden Paint Products, and our H-I-S products. However, we struggled to buy paint directly from Glidden and at the same time, be competitive with the box stores. The box stores undercut us, in that they were able to purchase Glidden paint at a lower cost than we were able to buy it. So in 1980, we closed the Midwest City store and I transferred to our location on 29 Street and Western as manager.

YOU LEARN BY DOING

In '83, I assumed the accounting responsibilities at H-I-S Paint, when a young lady, who had previously worked in this position, married and decided to start a family. That's where I found my niche – following in the footsteps of my Grandmother Cox and Grandfather Garrett, who both had both worked as accountants for car dealerships.

Computers were not widely available back then, so all the accounting functions were done manually. Like Dad, I learned from the school of hard knocks. I studied accounting at OSU-OKC, but the majority of my knowledge was learned through hands on-experience. Like Dad, I learned from the school of hard knocks.

Today, my official title is Vice President of Operations and CFO of H-I-S Coatings. My operations responsibilities include manufacturing, inventory management, product pricing and both customer and employee relations. A few of my financial responsibilities include: review of financial statements, cash flow, credit decisions, and other things of that nature.

In June 2001, I undertook the mammoth ISO 9001 certification process for H-I-S Paint: it involves all company suppliers used by H-I-S, client satisfaction surveys, employees at every level, and any entity our company does business with.

It is a set of policies, processes, and procedures required in the core business areas of a company to insure that the company is able to meet customer requirements. The key idea is to maintain product consistency. For example, when Dad orders a salad from a restaurant, he expects to receive the same salad he has ordered in the past, without variation. Being ISO 9001 Certified has given H-I-S creditability as we call on industrial customers across the United States.

Kirk's division is Architectural Sales, Tony's division is Industrial Sales, and I'm in Operations and Finance. This has allowed each of us to excel in our particular field without an overlap. Of course there have been ups and downs and at times, Dad has had to be the referee, but overall, it has worked out well both for us and for H-I-S. We meet monthly as a board, along with an outside consultant to make the company's major decisions.

CHARACTER IS FORMED BY CHOICES

Our company has implemented a monthly, companywide breakfast that we call "Character First." At the meeting, Dad gives a short devotional and talks about a character quality, followed by a specific example of how he has incorporated that quality into his life.

We also honor each employee on the anniversary month in which they began work with the company. Their supervisor gives a character quality he has observed in the individual and an example of how that employee demonstrates that character quality at H-I-S.

In addition, we honor each person's birthday month and give them a small bonus check. This has been an investment of both time and money, but it allows the people from all of our store locations to be together once a month, connect with each other, and catch up on the latest company news.

A few times after profitable years, Dad has handed out a bonus check or cash to each employee to let them know H-I-S values their service. It requires the combined effort of each individual employee to make the whole company a success.

DEVELOP A GOOD WORK ETHIC

As I look back, I appreciate that Dad instilled a work ethic in me by his exemplary example. When I was younger, he painted apartments and houses to help our family make ends meet. I think this is reflected in that we three brothers are all hard workers.

IF IT'S BROKEN, FIX IT

Dad is not a desk person—his expertise at H-I-S is in manufacturing processes and operations, and to this day, there is no one in the company who can walk through the production area and spot places for improvement better than Dad. His keen eye and discernment enable him to detect problems such as a machine whose sound isn't quite right. A sound no one else had noticed. And he is adamant in that if, something is broken, you get it fixed immediately.

KEEP IT CLEAN

He's also a stickler about the facilities maintenance: all areas must be clean and well organized. And there's another rule: if things cannot or have not been used, they need to be disposed of. Many, many visitors walk through our company and comment, "Your cleanliness is unusual for a paint company."

PRACTICE GENEROSITY

Another thing about Dad is his generosity. Numerous are the times I have seen him take money out of his pocket or write a check to help someone in need. He's a big supporter of his church, and Christian Heritage Academy, which is where his grandchildren attend, as well as other Christian organizations. Each year, H-I-S donates more financially to charities, the community, and other nonprofit organizations than can be written off our tax returns.

I don't know if common sense is something that can be taught or if it is inherited, but regardless of how he came by it, Dad definitely has it and I believe it has rubbed off on me. With his common-sense approach, I have watched him tackle anything from plumbing to electrical work, to fixing a car... really, anything to do with his hands. In return, watching him has challenged me to try things I might not otherwise have attempted.

TEACH WHAT YOU KNOW

In 2010, Dad and I were in Beijing, China where H-I-S now has a small paint factory. On this particular trip, our goal was to help them set up their manufacturing facility. With the help of an interpreter, Dad trained a guy, who spoke no English to make a batch of paint, quality control a batch of paint, and fill containers with paint just by his example. He could do that because he knew the process inside and out.

Demonstrating how to make paint.

The integrity of the upright will guide them, but the falseness of the treacherous will destroy them.

(Proverbs 11:3)

CHAPTER FORTY-TWO

REMEMBER WHERE YOU CAME FROM

Kirk

It seems like I've been around paint all my life. As I grew up, Dad has either worked for a paint company or owned a paint company. And many of my summer days, as a young grade-school-age kid, were spent playing in and around the first H-I-S Paint manufacturing plant located on High Street. My favorite pastime activities included: capturing scorpions, playing hide-and-seek around old bulk tanks, empty fifty-five gallon drums, and huge cardboard boxes, with the kids who lived next door to H-I-S.

I began work at H-I-S in '79 as a part-time employee while still in high school. I worked after school and in the summer months at the Midwest City store where I stocked paint, wallpaper, and assisted customers when needed.

After the decision was made to close the MWC store, I transferred to the location on 29 Street. More than just a store, it also became our manufacturing facility since we had earlier moved that aspect of the business from High Street to this location.

A glance back over those early years brings to mind a number of unique jobs that had to be done at the facility on 29 Street, no longer necessary today. As an upstart, small paint company, they were a necessary and essential part of H-I-S survival. Costs had to be watched and controlled at every turn.

One such job involved cotton. Huge, long rolls of it, rolls, that seemed to go on forever. We cut them into small, rag-size-pieces paint contractors could use for wiping their lacquer stains. These rolls were often the size of a small car, and we had to cut the roll into uniform, usable wiping rags, I weighed out ten-pound bundles and put it in a plastic bag. Precut, pre-packaged rags were a luxury we couldn't afford.

The most time-consuming job I recall was filling solvent buckets. Thinners and solvents were purchased in bulk, so we ran a hose from the bulk tank to fill the five- and one-gallon containers, which were sold in our paint stores. It was a lengthy, smelly process, but necessary, because we couldn't afford to buy the solvent prepackaged. We had to do it ourselves.

But by far, the hardest job for me, as a young boy was unloading semi trucks by hand. Our SW 29 Street factory and store did not have a loading dock, nor did we own a forklift, so whenever a big truck with a load of raw materials arrived, we had to unload it by hand. A job that, with a forklift would have taken a short amount of time, took well over an hour without one, and required a group effort of many. To handle and shoulder hundreds and hundreds of fifty-pound bags, can soon wear a person out.

These jobs are mentioned to remind us of those days because today, few H-I-S employees have a clue about the hard work that was required for our company to just survive. And survival was our goal. And we did what we had to do to that end.

Today, we no longer collect used buckets and pails, because we're able to buy new ones. And we purchase prepackaged solvents, wiping rags, and have several forklifts to do the heavy lifting at our loading docks.

These are reminders of the hard work of our past and where we came from . . . something I never want to forget. Dad had the brass, grit, and determination of an army mule. He did whatever it took to get the job done, to make his company a success, and didn't mind if he got dirty in the process, if that's what the job called for it. He tackles challenges and enjoys the reward of hard work.

When I started college, we moved our manufacturing facility from SW 29 Street to 1700 W. Sheridan, where I did a variety of jobs. I organized paint orders for walk-in customers, made deliveries, as well as delivered large orders to apartment complexes around town. In production, I washed the huge tanks we made paint in. While I never made a batch of paint, I helped the paint-makers who did.

After a batch of paint had been made, and passed the many laboratory quality control tests, it had to be packaged. Packaging involved moving the paint from

"Dad did whatever it took to get the job done, to make his company a success."

a huge five-hundred-gallon steel-mixing tub through a series of hoses, a strainer, and then into the one- and five-gallon containers. After the containers had been filled, labels and batch stickers had to be pasted to those containers, and lids hammered into place with a rubber mallet. Then we stacked those containers four or five buckets high onto a pallet, which was either added into inventory or placed on a truck for delivery.

One summer, I was assigned to the most brain-dead job a person could ever get. Data entry. That's where all the hand-written ticket information had to be typed into the computer. I hated it, but it was my fault. Due to my propensity to speed and wreck involvements, all of which resulted in too many tickets, the company's insurance coverage refused to insure me to drive a delivery truck. I was grounded for almost a year, and sequestered to data entry and production work, until I got the green light to drive again.

During this time, Dad decided it was time for me to learn sales. I spent one summer driving around with his sales guys. Each day, I rode around with a different sales rep and watched them, learned from them, questioned them, and received valuable on-the-job training.

I graduated in 1987 from the University of Oklahoma with a Bachelors of Business Administration Degree in both Marketing and Management. After which, I married Diane and went to work as a fulltime outside sales rep at H-I-S. I love sales.

I loved to go places. I loved to meet people. I loved the freedom. I loved the challenge. And the commission that came with it, worked for me too. Motivated and disciplined, sales turned out to be a breeze for me. With much to learn, thanks to Dad, the determination and work ethic was already there. He enrolled me in the Dale Carnegie Sales Training Course, which had proved beneficial for him.

Thanks to Dad and Uncle Johnny, we were now a major player in the property management market, but were weak in residential paint contractor and homebuilder markets. So these markets became my targeted focus. Our reputation had been earned in apartment paint sales, and we had yet to break that mindset. Our paint products were equivalent to and even better than the national brands used in these markets. Through hard work, determination, patience, and diligence our efforts paid off, and today, H-I-S Paint is a major player in these targeted markets.

In '92, Dad moved me into management as sales manager. And later, my role expanded to include that of sales representative. By '99, I assumed oversight responsibility of our three paint stores. At present, I am Vice-President Architectural Division at H-I-S Coatings. I work with and lead the architectural sales team, oversee leadership, planning, and expansion for the three H-I-S Coatings contractor/retail stores.

Blessed with a great sales team, exceptional store managers, employees and topnotch, quality products, our sales for this division has experienced a steady upward climb and we've been blessed with an expansion of new customers, new customer bases and markets.

One of the highlights of my career came when I traveled to China several times to work with H-I-S Coatings China. There I worked with and trained potential distributors, buyers, and customers on the various coatings that H-I-S Paint offered. While the hours are long and the work tedious, it's the element I thrive in. At the grand opening of a new H-I-S Paint store in China, I was honored to be the guest speaker. While there, I met many enthusiastic people, enjoyed their rich foreign culture, and have seen some of the wonders of the world, which together has given me many unforgettable experiences.

TOUGH TIMES ARE TEMPORARY BUT TRAITS LAST FOREVER

Dad taught me to be a hard worker, a risk-taker, and that no job is ever too big or too small. He taught me to multi-task, take initiative, and after a job is completed, to look for another and not wait for someone to point it out. A go-getter with initiative will look around, find something to do, and do it.

Dad taught me teamwork. You do whatever job is necessary to get the work or project completed. The phrase "That's not my job" is not in Dad's vocabulary. It never has been.

There isn't a job Dad feels is beneath him. He will find something to clean, or sweep in the warehouse, or drive a forklift, pick up trash, rearrange pallet racks or clean up an accidental spill. He's not the kind of guy who wears a suit and sits in his office all day. Matter of fact, he keeps a pair of old work clothes in his office just in case.

> "Dad taught me teamwork. You do whatever is necessary to ge the work or project completed."

Dad practices what he preaches and reads his Bible every day. He's a great boss, but an even better father. If I were to idolize someone, hands down, it's Dad. He taught me to be a leader, a manager, and to delegate. Over the years, I've watched him manage his employees, his business, and his life in general and have tried to follow his lead.

A righteous man who walks in his integrity—how blessed are his sons after him.

(Proverbs 20:7)

CHAPTER FORTY-THREE

FLYING COLORS

Tony

While I worked for H-I-S Paint in the summers and during high school since I was a boy, as I approached my senior year at the University of Oklahoma, I had no plans to work in the family business. But God had His plan. Through a series of career interviews and events, it became clear to me that God wanted me to work with Dad, and it has been an incredible journey. I've been blessed to build on the foundation he's laid for his sons and future generations, and to be a part of the work environment he's created which reflects his godly character. A culture that I pray will be embraced by the next generation.

Like Kirk, I graduated from the University of Oklahoma with degrees in both Bachelors of Business Administration and Marketing and after a few job interviews with other companies, decided to join the family business as a sales rep in '87. Today I'm the Vice President of Industrial Coating.

A greenhorn, fresh from the University, I jumped into the company with both feet and attempted to implement my textbook knowledge of organizational structure and management complete with charts.

In a Monday morning meeting, I presented my ideas to Dad, my brothers, and some of the key employees at a local corner café called Hogan's. Dad gave me a quick lesson. He said that respect had to be earned and dues paid if my ideas were to merit consideration. After the meeting, Dad told me to hit the street and prove myself if I wanted to gain the respect of my fellow employees and expect them to listen to my ideas.

So, hit the streets I did, traveling around the city and state: I called on residential and commercial contractors, apartments, hotels, schools, housing authorities, military bases, oilfield yards, and industrial fabricators. I learned that potential clients needed product information and literature—not just a salesman with paint prices. But business cards and price sheets were all we had; we had no product data literature, paint systems, catalogs, or any type of marketing information. If we were to grow and reach new markets, we needed literature for potential clients along with pricing.

The first generation of Mac computers available for use at Kinko's came in handy. We designed labels, wrote product literature, and provided whatever else might be needed to support our direct sales efforts.

Branding was another challenge. Who was H-I-S Paint? Most people had never heard of our company or our paint brand, and for those who had used our product, our brand image was simple; quality and value at a low price with incredible service. Regardless of our efforts in the commercial market, H-I-S was either not on their specs or we were just an apartment paint to the big fish in town, who used PPG, Sherwin Williams, and Kelly Moore. A recognition and credibility battle lurked around every corner. That is the only way I can explain those first ten years in sales.

Our annual ad in the Yellow Pages was the extent of our advertisement efforts up to this time. And Dad was a big believer in the Yellow Pages. To strengthen our brand, we needed exposure in different media. We needed name recognition if we were to attract potential customers—customers willing to give us an opportunity to earn their business.

Thus began the arduous job of market transition within H-I-S Paint. We made the leap from a "product-oriented" focus with a few paint products to a "market-oriented" focus with branding and custom formulating. Our need to market and advertise was greater than the current success we now had through direct sales without it and by '93, six years after my brother, Kirk, and I joined the company, our direct sales efforts, supplemented by minimal marketing efforts, had almost doubled the company's revenues.

With a few multi-million dollar revenue years under my belt in direct sales, I felt I had earned the right to direct and shore up our market efforts.

Over the next several years, we expanded from direct sales to a focus, which included development into tradeshow booths as well as branding to various industries. We created advertisement campaigns and jingles to blast our brand's message across radio and TV airwaves. A graphics department was established to develop professional labels, logos, and coatings systems to market our literature. This enabled us to pursue specification approvals and satisfy the information requirements our target markets needed.

We also developed a mission statement, which can be found in the Appendix of this book.

The shift in our focus to market expansion enabled us to open new stores in the Lawton and Tulsa markets, which included additional market-focused reps as well as a minor focus into the industrial Original Equipment Manufacturing market.

"Dad knew his success was from the Lord, and if his company was to survive for the next generation, he needed resources and wise council."

The greatest catalyst for change began in '97. Dad knew his success was from the Lord, and if his company was to survive for the next generation, he needed resources and wise counsel. A friend, Jim Daniels, invited Dad to attend a presentation offered by a Professional Resource

Group, whose focus was to prepare family-owned companies for long-term generational success.

To maintain our momentum, Dad hired skilled people, invested in the finest equipment and expanded our facilities. And he retained the strategic planner from the Professional Resource Group to implement those changes.

With God's help and Dad's leadership, H-I-S Paint now services some of the biggest names in manufacturing. In 2012, we shipped products to thirty-eight states and eight countries. Today, the company competes in the global marketplace with revenues well above our expectations. And we give God all the glory, for we recognize that without Him, we could do nothing.

When I reflect on Dad's life since his conversion, I see a man who is fruitful and effective. I see a man, who made a life decision to build upon his faith, and worked to add virtue and love as II Peter 1:5-8 instructs. Some Christian men may add a fair amount of virtue and knowledge to their lives after their conversion, but few measure up to Dad.

After his life change, I remember Dad as determined and steadfast, and he did his best to change our family values while working through his own demons. He made a concerted effort to make up for lost time through family vacations, and sporting events. And the conflicts between him and Mom diminished as he learned to love and serve her as God instructs. In addition, he worked hard to provide for his family and make the company profitable. Our church also found itself recipients of Dad's life change. He poured his life into it while at the same evangelizing Christ's message. Invest your time and talents with eternity in mind.

For this very reason, make every effort to supplement your faith with virtue, and virtue with knowledge, and knowledge with self-control, and self-control with steadfastness, and steadfastness with godliness, and godliness with brotherly affection, and brotherly affection with love. (II Peter 1:5-8 ESV)

Tony, Joe, Kirk, my dad, Carl, & Kent

CHAPTER FORTY-FOUR

LESSON IN HUMILITY

The Southwestern Paint and Coatings Association regularly held their annual joint conventions either in Dallas or Houston, which I had attended with previous employers. It was a conference I enjoyed, because it showcased the latest in new equipment and raw materials.

In '77, the convention was in Dallas, and a supplier invited me to play golf with him at a very nice country club. Dorothy traveled with me to these conventions, but since the golf game was scheduled for Wednesday, the day before the convention started, I decided to fly down a day early, and Dorothy planned to drive down the next day.

During the flight, as I looked out the window and marveled at the beautiful white clouds and blue sky, I thought to myself... *you have arrived.*

We landed at the Dallas/Ft. Worth Airport, where I proceeded to collect my golf bag and luggage. But when I reached the cabstand, there were no cab drivers, because the cab drivers were all on strike. The only alternative was to find a city bus to take me to the Hilton Hotel on Mockingbird Lane where I had reservations.

Not long after boarding the bus, which I thought would transport me to the Hilton, the driver pulled into the bus lot on Coit Road and Interstate 635 and parked. I had failed to notice that I was the only person on the bus, and when the bus driver began to exit the bus, I asked him, "Why have you stopped?"

He replied, "I'm going home."

To which I said, "Home, you can't go home. What about me?"

I told him of my predicament, and my sore need of a ride to the Hilton, so he agreed to drive me in his car. When we arrived at the Hilton, I presented my confirmation number, and discovered that my room had been given away due to my late arrival. It was midnight. No cab. No room. And I thought I had arrived.

A friend was staying in the hotel, so I called his room to see if I could stay with him. He said he had a woman in the room for the night, so that was not an option. I told the hotel clerk of my dilemma and pleaded for his help. He located a locked-off portion of a room with a small bed that pulled down from the wall.

God knows just how to handle pride. And that night I found out I wasn't as important as I thought I was.

Before long, I realized the lesson God had in mind: my pride was being called out. Don't think that I won some big victory that day. I didn't. I just recognized how far I had yet to go. I was—and still am—learning to stay humble. If you

> **"And that night, I found out I wasn't as important as I thought I was."**

think I have it all together, you'd be wrong. However, I admit to the sin no one wants to admits to. Humility has an enemy called pride.

Why don't we want to admit we are prideful? Well . . . because our pride is usually the foundation of our struggles.

The real reason we get our feelings hurt, why we hate being passed over for a promotion, why we feel rejection, why we continue to refuse to admit our mistakes, why we care more about what others think than we do our character, the driving force behind wanting to receive the credit for something, holding grudges, and being jealous is pride.

Pride is what makes us do what we do.

The Bible has nothing good to say about pride. Pride has many names in Scripture: arrogance, smug, superior. It is seen as narcissism, conceit, ego, or self-importance.

Simply put, pride is the opposite of humility.

As I write this, I pray you will be driven to be more like Jesus. Jesus was never proud or arrogant. He never tried to make others feel inferior. No matter how we struggle with pride, we can begin to follow Jesus' example.

The Bible tells us to have the same attitude Jesus had. He thought of others as more important than Himself, He was concerned with their needs more than His own.

Pride competes with humility. Pride wants to hold center-stage and talk more than listen, while humility listens; pride takes offense while humility inspires harmony; pride is stubborn while humility seeks the good of others. Let humility win. Humility says, "Dear God, I need your help." Pride wants to be independent, but we are to be completely dependent on God.

My lesson in humility reminded me of 1Peter 5:5, "… for God is opposed to the proud, but gives grace to the humble." Humility means to know we are nothing without God, and that all the good things happen because of God. My life has not been without its struggles. But I found freedom when I faced the fact that I could not work out my problems without Him.

Humility does not mean to put your self down. Instead, it means to know that God will always do what is in your best interest, if you will trust His character. We can disarm pride and walk in peace, when we learn to live like this.

Pride goes before destruction, and a haughty spirit before stumbling. (Proverbs 16:18)

CHAPTER FORTY-FIVE

FAN DECK

Nothing I have achieved could have been done without the investments of others in my life.

A fan deck is made up of a selection of 1,300 colors printed on two-inch by nine-inch cards, which are held together by a single bolt at one end of the collection, and it's called a fan deck because it can be spread out like a fan to display all the colors at once. My life is like that fan deck, but instead of colors, it is made up of people from all different backgrounds with different

skill sets and abilities, and each of them bring color into my life. This chapter is my fan deck of people who have influenced and blessed me over the years.

Since the day I was born, whether I knew it or not, God had a plan for me. The tapestry analogy is a good description of His work in a person's life. While the front side appears to be a beautiful, masterfully woven scene, a look at the backside reveals a jumbled mess of knots, loose threads, and confusion. That accurately describes my life.

As I write this, my wife Dorothy and I have been married for fifty-five years. God, in His perfect plan, put us together. She's a wonderful wife and mother. I love her. She's my best friend. And most of the time, we even think alike. We enjoy the same things like: teaching a class at church, watching our grandchildren participate in school events, playing a round of golf together, attending Thunder basketball games, attending University of Oklahoma football games, or walking alone on the beach together.

When I look at our family portrait, I think to myself, O Lord, my how You have multiplied and blessed our family. We have thirteen grandchildren and seven great grandchildren.

Our complete family in July 2013.

Unless the Lord builds the house, they labor in vain who build it. (Psalm 127:1)

Ronald E. Kozak,
Strategic Business Planning Consultant
and Corporate Coach

As a business consultant, I started working with H-I-S Paint in July 1998. With Joe Cox's leadership and the support of his three sons, Kent, Kirk, and Tony, along with Steve Bussjaeger, the Management Team developed a Strategic Plan to take the Company to the next level.

However, there is more to the H-I-S story than the making and selling of paint. There are many companies that profess and advertise the fact that they are "Christian companies" only to be seen later as anything but that. I have personally seen Christian beliefs in action where the actions always speak louder and more profoundly than words. Customers and employees have benefited from this belief structure where customers and customer relationships always come first.

Employees who come forward with personal troubles at H-I-S Paint are offered help through professional counseling or other forms of support, as long as the employee is willing to change and makes an effort to improve themselves. This creates a win for both the employee and the company.

Is H-I-S a "laissez-faire" environment where employees are allowed to do whatever they want? No, all employees, family included, are expected to work and contribute to the success of the company at all levels. Honoring people's efforts, as well as their significant character traits through our Character First program, is a major part of recognizing the important role each person has to play.

In conclusion, I want to thank you, Joe Cox, for allowing me to have a small part in your forty-year-old success story. I know your legacy of Christian values will continue to be played out through your sons and H-I-S will continue to be known as an authentic Christian company.

APPENDIX

*SEVEN MINUTES WITH GOD, HOW TO PLAN A DAILY QUIET TIME (NavPress, a Ministry of the Navigators) by Robert Foster (1997).

*H-I-S Paint Company's Mission Statement:
We provide our customers with the highest quality coatings and strive to be the benchmark standard in customer service. We work to maintain the utmost level of integrity in all relationships, and provide a work environment that allows our employees to meet their fullest potential. We seek to proclaim a Christian worldview of God's faithfulness to all.

Scripture Index

Below is a list of all the verses I used in this book to tell my story. These verses are far more than just sayings, or ideas – they are game-changers. To experience the full impact of these verses, get a Bible in a translation you can understand, look up each reference, and read the whole chapter where the verse is found. While reading, ask yourself, "What is the simple truth of this chapter?" Write your answer next to each verse below.

Chapter 1: Psalm 62:12

Chapter 2: Proverbs 27:17

Chapter 3: Proverbs 17:10

Chapter 4: Proverbs 17:22, Proverbs 22:6

Chapter 5: Proverbs 16:25

Chapter 6: Proverbs 18:9

Chapter 7: Proverbs 15:21

Chapter 8: Proverbs 16:2

Chapter 9: Psalm 90:14

Chapter 10: Genesis 2:24

Chapter 11: II Timothy 1:7 (KJV)

Chapter 12: Proverbs 15:16

Chapter 13: II Timothy 2:3 (KJV)

Chapter 14: Proverbs 6:23

Chapter 15: Ecclesiastes 4:13

Chapter 16: Proverbs 16:17

Chapter 17: Proverbs 22:3

Chapter 18: John 8:12, Psalm 42:11 (KJV)

Chapter 19: Galatians 6:9

Chapter 20: Galatians 6:8

Chapter 21: Proverbs 22:26-27, Proverbs 20:1 (KJV)

Chapter 22: Proverbs 10:17

Chapter 23: Proverbs 21:17, Psalm 91:14 (KJV), Joshua 24:15 (KJV)

Chapter 24: John 3:16, Romans 10:9-10, Galatians 5:20-21, Daniel 9:9

Chapter 25: James 1:12

Chapter 26: Proverbs 22:2, John 15:5

Chapter 27: Zechariah 4:10, Proverbs 6:6-11, Philippians 4:19

Chapter 28: Psalm 58:11

Chapter 29: I Corinthians 10:13, Matthew 26:41 (KJV)

Chapter 30: Proverbs 10:4

Chapter 31: I Samuel 16:7

Chapter 32: Romans 8:28, John 14:6, Proverbs 22:1, Job 34:21, Psalm 37:23

Chapter 33: Proverbs 18:22, Proverbs 31:30

Chapter 34: I Samuel 15:23, Ephesians 5:22-25, Proverbs 6:23

Chapter 35: Psalm 37:4

Chapter 36: Romans 3:23, John 3:16, Romans 10:9-10, Philippians 1:6

SEVEN MINUTES WITH GOD:
HOW TO PLAN A DAILY QUIET TIME
By Robert D. Foster

The intimacy of communion with Christ must be recaptured in the morning quiet time. Call it what you want—quiet time, personal devotions, the morning watch, or individual worship- these holy minutes at the start of each day explain the inner secret of Christianity. It's the golden thread that ties every great man of God together- from Moses to David Livingstone, the prophet Amos to Billy Graham- rich and poor, businessmen and military personnel. Every man who ever became somebody for God has this at the core of his priorities: time alone with God.

David says in Psalm 56:7 "My heart is fixed." A fixed and established heart produces stability in life. Few men in the Christian community have this heart and life. A vital link is needed to maintain your morning watch and that is the development of a workable plan. It will help you to be consistent.

I want to suggest that in order to get under way, you start with seven minutes. Perhaps you could call it a daily "Seven-Up." Five minutes may be too short, and ten minutes for some is a little too long at first.

Will you take seven minutes every day? Not five mornings out of seven, not six days out of seven- but seven days out of seven. Ask God to help you: "Lord, I want to meet you the first thing in my day for at least seven minutes. Tomorrow when the alarm clock goes off at 6:15 A.M., I have an appointment with you."

Your prayer might be, "Morning by morning, O Lord, You hear my voice; morning by morning I lay my requests before You and wait in expectation." (Psalm 5:3)

How do you spend these seven minutes? After getting out of bed and taking care of your personal needs, you will want to find a quiet place and there with your Bible enjoy the solitude of seven minutes with God.

Invest the first 30 seconds preparing your heart. Thank Him for the good night of sleep and the opportunities of this new day. "Lord, cleanse my heart so You can speak to me through the scriptures. Open my heart. Fill my heart. Make my mind alert, my soul active, and my heart responsive. Lord, surround me with Your presence during this time. Amen."

Now take four minutes to read the Bible. Your greatest need is to hear some word from God. Allow the word to strike fire in your heart. Meet the Author.

One of the Gospels is a good place to begin reading. Start with the Book of Mark. Read consecutively - every verse, chapter after chapter. Don't race, but avoid stopping to do a Bible study on some word, thought, or theological problem, which presents itself. Read for the pure joy of reading, and allow God to speak— perhaps just 20 verses, or maybe a complete chapter. When you have finished Mark start the Gospel of John. Soon you'll want to go ahead and read the entire New Testament.

After God has spoken through His Book, then speak to Him — in prayer. You have two and half minutes left for fellowship with Him in four areas of prayer that you can remember by the word ACTS.

A- Adoration. This is the purest kind of prayer because it's all for God—there's nothing in it for you. You don't barge into the presence of royalty. You begin with the proper salutation. So worship Him. Tell the Lord that you love Him. Reflect on His greatness, His power, His majesty, and sovereignty.

C- Confession follows. Having seen Him you now want to be sure every sin is cleansed and forsaken. Confession comes from a root word meaning "to agree together with." Apply this to prayer. It means to agree with God. Something happened yesterday you called a slight exaggeration - God call's it a lie! You call it strong language- God calls it swearing. You call it telling the truth about somebody in the church- God calls it gossip. "If I regard iniquity in my heart, the Lord will not hear me." (Psalm 66:18)

T- Thanksgiving. Express your gratitude to God. Think of several specific things to thank Him for: your family, your business, your church and ministry responsibilities- even thank Him for hardships. "In everything give thanks: for this is the will of God in Christ Jesus concerning you" (I Thessalonians 5:18)

S- Supplication. This means to "ask for, earnestly and humbly." This is the part of your prayer life where you make your petitions known to Him. Ask for others, then for yourself. Why not include other people around the world, such as missionaries, students studying abroad, friends in distant places, and above all the people of many lands who have yet to hear about Jesus Christ. Let's put these seven minutes together:

> 0:30   Prayer for guidance (Psalm 143:8)
> 4:00   Reading the Bible (Psalm 119:18)
> 2:30   Prayer:
>   Adoration (I Chronicles 29:11)
>   Confession (I John 1:19)
>   Thanksgiving (Ephesians 5:20)
>   Supplication (Matthew 7:7)

This is simply a guide. Soon you will discover that it is impossible to spend only seven minutes with the Lord. An amazing thing happens – seven minutes become 20, and it's not long before you're spending 30 precious minutes with Him. Do not become devoted to the habit, but to the Savior.

Do it not because other men are doing it- not as a spiritless duty every morning, nor merely as an end in itself, but because God has granted the priceless privilege of fellowship with HIMSELF. Covenant with Him now to guard, nourish, and maintain your morning watch of seven minutes.

Epilogue

It's time to quit watching the paint dry.

Expressions get old because they've been around a long time; and they've been around a long time usually because they are true. They've been time-tested and found to be true for every generation. One such expression is "watching paint dry."

From my years in the paint business, I understand the literal meaning of this phrase. "Watching paint dry" means waiting until it's completely dry before adding another coat or moving on to the next job. Is watching paint dry necessary?

It is, believe it or not. It requires an expert watcher who knows what to look for, to see if the color darkens while it's drying or if the paint shrinks and cracks. The drying of paint is a very exact science and can be the difference of a job poorly done or a job well done.

Paint takes about two hours to dry completely, and it's something only time can take care of, so you need to be patient. When standing idle or doing nothing for long periods of time, the two-hour process of watching paint dry can suddenly feel much longer.

Some people have used this expression to describe an activity, which is found to be laborious, uninteresting, or tedious. "Ugh, this is so boring—I'd rather watch paint dry." But there is another usage for this common idiom—it describes the passive state of a person. It describes a person who has become a-bystander to their own existence. That person's life has become humdrum. Blah. Dead. Boring.

Why? Because we are not born to be spectators of life but participants! Watching the paint dry means we are watching life happen around us and happening to us while we stand by and do nothing. Like paint fastening to a wall, our character is formed and our destiny shaped while we stand at a distance as onlookers.

I once heard a story of a guy who had spent most of his life knocking around the country working odd jobs at ski resorts and golf clubs. This guy had come from a wealthy family, had been provided a good education and grown up surrounded by luxury, but now was a man without purpose and direction. He had everything to live with but nothing to live for. He was watching the paint dry on his life.

One day he found himself working out in the same local gym as an oil executive, who saw potential in this young man. The executive walked over, introduced himself, and said, "It's about time."

"For what?" the young man replied.

"About time to get your life together and get on with living," the executive said.

It was a turning point in this young man's life, and became the motivation he needed to stop watching the paint dry and begin to live the life he was designed to live.

This is what I want to say to you: Isn't it about time you stopped watching the paint dry and do something with the time and life you've been given? No matter who you are or how old you are or where you're from or what's happened in your life, my challenge is the same.

If you've built a company, made money, raised a family, and own nice things, then don't stagnate in your success: living to buy more things and gain more square footage. Instead, find a way to leverage your accomplishments to help others.

If you're just beginning your career, then my hope is that you will work with eternity in mind. How tragic it would be to climb the ladder of success only to discover that ladder has been leaning against the wrong wall.

As I write this, I think about what I would say to my grandkids and their friends. Something like this:

People around you aren't always going to be there to make your life work or to get you out of problems. You are not owed success because of your family, and neither are you entitled to live carelessly, squandering your time, talents, and gifts. Jesus said it best when He said, "To whom much is given, much is required."

Don't let life happen to you; instead, you happen to life. Take time to seek God's will, pray about your purpose, and dream about what could be if God really had his way In your life.

My message to you is: "ISN'T IT ABOUT TIME YOU STOP WATCHING THE PAINT DRY AND BEGIN LIVING?"

July 2013